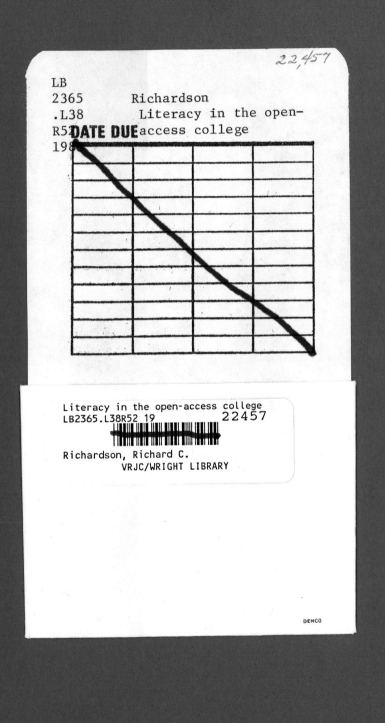

❧ ❧ ❧

Literacy
in the Open-Access
College

❧ ❧ ❧

Richard C. Richardson, Jr.

Elizabeth C. Fisk

Morris A. Okun

Literacy in the Open-Access College

Jossey-Bass Publishers

San Francisco • Washington • London • 1983

LITERACY IN THE OPEN-ACCESS COLLEGE
by Richard C. Richardson, Jr., Elizabeth C. Fisk,
and Morris A. Okun

Copyright © 1983 by: Jossey-Bass Inc., Publishers
433 California Street
San Francisco, California 94104
&
Jossey-Bass Limited
28 Banner Street
London EC1Y 8QE

Library of Congress Cataloging in Publication Data

Richardson, Richard C.
    Literacy in the open-access college.

    Bibliography: p. 171
    Includes index.
    1. Language arts (Higher)—United States—Case studies.
2. Community colleges—United States—Open admission—
Case studies. 3. Community colleges—United States—
Curricula—Case studies. I. Fisk, Elizabeth C. II. Okun,
Morris A. III. Title.
LB2365.L38R52   1982   378'.052   83-11999
ISBN 0-87589-569-7

Manufactured in the United States of America

The paper in this book meets the guidelines for
permanence and durability of the Committee on
Production Guidelines for Book Longevity of the
Council on Library Resources.

JACKET DESIGN BY WILLI BAUM

FIRST EDITION

Code 8316

⚜ ⚜ ⚜

Preface

⚜ ⚜ ⚜

In 1960, Burton Clark published *The Open Door College,* a case study of San Jose City College. The book described an institution dedicated to the principle that no individual eighteen years of age or older should be denied the opportunity to attempt a college education regardless of aptitude or previous academic preparation. The concept of an institution designed to help the disadvantaged help themselves through the great American equalizer, education, was a perfect fit for our national aspirations during the "Great Society" decade of the sixties. Community colleges became the embodiment of the concept of "open door" institutions and by mid-decade were being established at the rate of one a week.

The primary objective of community leaders and legislators who worked to establish these open-door colleges was to provide the first two years of the standard baccalaureate sequence. In addition, these leaders recognized the necessity of providing an alternative in the form of terminal one- or two-year occupational programs for those who were uninterested in or unable to pursue the bachelor's degree. The notion that such institutions would eventually become involved in extensive remedial work, duplicating programs previously associated with the public schools, was as far from the thoughts of founders as the idea that such colleges would eventually become major competitors of YMCAs and related community agencies in providing leisure time activities.

The concept of using the open-door college as a tool for addressing inequities in social status or income was a noble one. By mid-decade, however, the disparities between concept and practice had become evident. The first wave of criticism focused on the high drop-out rates of underprepared students, suggesting that the open-door should be renamed the revolving door. Closely following the first wave was a second and more serious charge. The social critics, including Karabel (1972, 1974) and Jencks and Riesman (1968), built on Clark's (1960) "cooling out" observations to allege that open-door colleges perpetuated social inequities by introducing a tracking system into American higher education.

In the decade of the seventies, a series of events overtook the open-door colleges. Dissatisfied with the growing concentration of minorities in community colleges, civil rights leaders worked for open admissions at four-year colleges and universities. Initially, the response was to recruit talented minority students, defined as those possessing the same academic characteristics as their majority counterparts. It soon became apparent, however, that an historically separate and unequal system of public education could not produce anywhere near the number of academically prepared minority students that affirmative action guidelines suggested should now be enrolled in four-year colleges and universities. The outcome was predictable. Selective institutions developed new admission procedures that enrolled students unprepared to meet their academic requirements. For the first time in more than a decade, selective universities and four-year colleges offered remedial instruction.

Hard on the heels of affirmative action came the bad news of demographic projections. Those parts of the nation served by the largest number of four-year colleges and universities were faced with decreases of up to 40 percent in their traditional college-age population. Many institutions reacted like soldiers going into battle: the bullets would strike somewhere else. By 1980, however, many colleges had experienced enrollment declines.

Enter the age of marketing. The philosophic commitment of the sixties to provide opportunity through *open doors* had been transformed into the legal and economic imperatives of the eighties to provide *open access* through adjusting admission requirements to meet affirmative action guidelines and to ensure institutional survival. The open-access college of the eighties, in contrast to its open-door predecessor, is as likely to be four-year as two-year. Because the traditional opportunity function of the two-year college has increasingly been assumed by four-year institutions, two-year colleges have been pressured to seek new missions and an ever more diverse clientele. Unlike the open-door colleges, open-access institutions in general, and community colleges in particular, believe in lifelong learning and gear their educational programs to the demands of the marketplace rather than to traditional views of what ought to comprise a college education. In practice, this belief translates into a willingness to provide virtually any educational program to almost any clientele provided someone is willing to supply the necessary funding.

Because the community college is the prototype of the open-access institution, it was chosen by our interdisciplinary team of researchers at Arizona State University as the appropriate site for studying the effects of open access on institutions and their students. Our study focused on literacy development, recognizing that critical reading and writing skills distinguish the educated and educable from the undereducated and the functionally illiterate. This book reports a three-year study of one open-access community college given the pseudonym of Oakwood.

Consistent with information available about community colleges nationwide (Cohen and Brawer, 1982), we saw little evidence at Oakwood that extensive reading or writing demands were placed on students. Obviously absent were forms and genres of written language earlier considered typical of college work: term papers, essay exams, and required reading lists were rare. The issues raised by our study, however, go beyond a concern for preserving traditional forms of written language or requiring a minimum amount of reading and writing, as has been suggested by recent critics of the literacy "crisis" (Coppermann, 1978). In fact, current views of literacy suggest that language use should be expected to change as society changes and as communication technology advances. No research supports the contention that collegiate forms of reading and writing *in and of themselves* are essential to learning or effective participation in modern society (Graff, 1979). Yet the literacy we observed involved more than the absence of traditional forms and quantity; it revealed a lack of emphasis on *critical literacy,* long considered the hallmark of collegiate study. Critical literacy, while not necessarily linked to specific forms of written language, *does* require clear articulation of educational goals and the development of high levels of thinking. It requires independence and self-direction.

Rather than reflecting critical literacy, Oakwood students' use of written language indicated dependence on instructors and staff. We labeled the literacy promoted in the classroom as instrumental "bitting" because it involved the transfer of preselected bits of information without requiring analysis, synthesis, or original expression. For example, note taking had become a mechanical procedure of copying words and brief phrases from the blackboard in order to recognize these bits on multiple choice tests. Students acted as consumers of language rather than as authors or critics.

The prevalence of bitting can be traced to several factors, among them the lack of an integrated curriculum and the absence of effective student advising. The priorities of administrators, concerned primarily with growth and community demands for relevant courses, did not include literacy development and seemed indirectly to promote bitting. The modal student at Oakwood attended part-time and was strikingly different in preparation and motivations from students who predominated in the middle sixties when the college was founded. The modal faculty member was also a part-time participant with allegiances to other employers and interests. In the classroom, these part-time students and instructors had complementary goals focused on the transfer of basic factual knowledge. Written language functioned as a tool to accomplish this transfer as efficiently as possible. Over time, demands for more critical reading and writing activities were dropped since they were inefficient and inappropriate to student and instructor goals.

Because they lacked well-articulated educational goals, Oakwood students showed little resemblance to self-directed learners who might be expected to respond to rapid changes in their jobs or to opportunities for advanced education and training. Students' experiences at the college reinforced their role as consumers of prepackaged learning. The bitting form of reading and writing they displayed, while reflecting a lack of critical literacy, appeared to be the socially appropriate behavior. To the extent that colleges like Oakwood continue to emphasize this dependent student role, they risk producing citizens who are underprepared for job advancement or social change.

From the perspective of our study, however, we suggest that open-access colleges cannot promote standards for critical literacy without extensive change. Admission policies, standards for academic progress, financial aid practices, and approaches to remediation are among the areas needing change. The majority of educationally and economically disadvantaged students in higher education are enrolled in open-access community colleges. The failure to enhance critical literacy in such institutions creates a credibility crisis that may undermine gains of the past two decades in opening access to postsecondary education.

More than thirty people contributed to the research on which this book is based. They helped to clarify design issues; interviewed faculty members, students, and administrators; conducted observations throughout the campus; and participated in the endless meetings through which data were evaluated and interpreted. Those who participated in the project are named in the technical report we prepared for the National Institute of Education (Richardson and others, 1982), and our gratitude goes to each of them. In particular, we wish to thank Kathryn Martens, Keith Thomas, and Elizabeth Brandt, whose counsel, patience, and hard work were indispensable to the conduct of the research and the preparation of the technical report. Their contributions helped to make this book possible. We are indebted to Art Cohen who read the manuscript and provided much helpful criticism.

We are also grateful to Dorla Nelson who typed and retyped chapter drafts when even word-processing equipment proved inadequate to the magnitude of revisions. She was ably assisted by Pamela Hanfelt and Dolores Shelby.

This book is dedicated to the administrators, faculty members, and students of Oakwood Community College, whose cooperation during months and years of observing, questioning, and reporting was essential to the success of the research. We hope the following pages convey the high respect we developed for individual and collective efforts to cope with the most complex and challenging educational issues of our day. We chose Oakwood for our study because we believed it was an excellent institution in the mainstream of the American community college movement. We saw nothing during our study to cause us to question this initial judgment.

We deeply appreciate the support of the National Institute of Education and, in accordance with the terms of our contract, advise readers that *the work on which this publication is based was performed pursuant to contract 400-78-0061 with the Teaching/Learning Division of the National Institute of Education and does not necessarily reflect the views of that agency.* (A complete report of the three-year research project is available through the ERIC Document Reproduction Service No. ED 217 925.)

Tempe, Arizona   Richard C. Richardson, Jr.
June 1983   Elizabeth C. Fisk
                                                              Morris A. Okun

Contents

The Authors

Richard C. Richardson, Jr., is professor and chair of the Department of Higher and Adult Education at Arizona State University. He received his bachelor's degree (1954) in education from Castleton State College, his master's degree (1958) in education from Michigan State University, and his doctor's degree (1963) in college administration from the University of Texas at Austin, where he was named a distinguished graduate of the College of Education in 1982. He also holds an honorary doctorate from Lafayette. He has served on the boards of the American Association of Community and Junior Colleges, the American Council on Education, and the American Association for Higher Education. Interested in community colleges and organizational theory, his previous work includes *Governance for the Two-Year College* (1972) and *The Two-Year College: A Social Synthesis* (1965).

Richardson was president of Northampton County Area Community College in Bethlehem, Pennsylvania (1967-1977), and dean of instruction at St. Louis Community College at Forest Park (1964-1967).

Elizabeth C. Fisk is assistant professor of education at Arizona State University. She received her bachelor's degree (1970) in psychology from Brandeis University and her master's degree (1971) in education from Harvard University. She recently completed her doctoral work (1982) in education at Arizona State University while serving as research assistant and university fellow. Fisk has coauthored several articles on adult learning, literacy, and qualitative research and has had professional experience as instructor and staff developer in a variety of programs—including adult basic education, developmental studies, and English as a second language.

Morris A. Okun is associate professor of education at Arizona State University. He received his bachelor's degree (1971) from Brooklyn College of the City University of New York and his master's and doctor's degrees (1973 and 1975) in educational psychology from Pennsylvania State University. From 1975 through 1976, he served as postdoctoral fellow at the Center for the Study of Aging and Human Development at Duke Medical Center. An educational psychologist and adult developmental psychologist by training, Okun has written numerous articles on adult learning and motivation. His current research focuses on the determinants of subjective well-being in adulthood.

❧ ❧ ❧

Literacy
in the Open-Access
College

❧ ❧ ❧

CHAPTER ONE

❧ ❧ ❧

Changing Concepts of Literacy

❧ ❧ ❧

Over the past twenty years, the community college has spearheaded the movement from meritocratic to mass higher education. Now, because of declining numbers of students of traditional college age and the postsecondary system's commitment to unending growth, many comprehensive public colleges and universities, as well as less visible private colleges, are on the brink of open access.

Changes in the characteristics of those matriculating are only one part of the picture. Once admitted, a more diverse clientele has exerted steady pressure on curriculum and teaching methods (Boyer and Hechinger, 1981). Grading procedures have been altered in many open-access colleges to allow withdrawal through the last day of class without penalty. As a result, those who would fail at college simply withdraw and, if they wish, return the following semester. Financial aid policies have placed pressure on institutions to broaden the definition of courses that may be counted for degree credit. Colleges need students to fund their budgets, and students need financial aid to remain in college. The failure of many open-access institutions to monitor their students' progress has led to public skep-

1

ticism about institutions' concern for students as learners, as contrasted with students as sources of revenue to fuel the institutions' continuing growth. Attendance of large numbers of non-degree-earning students has led to a deemphasis on advanced courses. Thus, somewhat ironically, institutional characteristics actually inhibit a degree candidate's ability to persist to graduation, once regarded as the only valid reason for attending.

In the early sixties, the movement from meritocratic to universal higher education was undertaken with the notion that it would be a "leveling up" process. Those from the disadvantaged segments of society would be given the tools they required to make themselves competitive, reducing social and economic differences. The question now is whether the democratization of higher education has been achieved by leveling up the disadvantaged sectors or by "leveling down" the opportunities previously available only to more advantaged groups of learners. To the extent that these opportunities are leveled down, they become less valuable both to advantaged and disadvantaged students.

Probably, the area of competence most affected by the leveling down process has been literacy. As the college experience becomes less differentiated from everyday life, standards of literate behavior come to approximate the standards that prevail in society at large. This book documents the leveling down of literacy observed during a three-year study at one open-access college, given the pseudonym of Oakwood. More important, the study identifies key variables for any strategy of intervention to reverse current trends toward declining literacy requirements. Although the book is based primarily on the results of the Oakwood study conducted by Richardson and others (1982), the findings of related studies of literacy in other community colleges, as well as a variety of contemporary settings, have been incorporated.

The Oakwood study used a naturalistic approach to research. There have been several naturalistic or quasi-naturalistic studies of the community college (London, 1978; Zwerling, 1976; Clark, 1960), but the Oakwood study was unique in the complexity, duration, and depth of its data collection. Data were collected with great intensity over a two-year period, and numerous researchers contributed. In none of the major areas of interest (administration, student support services, and instruction) did we rely on the observations or perspectives of a single person. Although the numbers involved posed enormous problems of coordination and analysis, they contributed significantly to the validity and reliability of the results. By balancing the differing perspectives of students, faculty members, and administrators against the views of researchers, we could identify the changes taking place with respect to literacy demands as well as the variables contributing to the reduction in emphasis on critical reading and writing.

Our in-depth study of one community college highlights the dynamic interplay of factors influencing literacy in this setting. Of course, we make no claim that the college we studied is representative of all community colleges. However, many of our findings are consistent with data from recent national and regional surveys, as well as other case studies of single institutions. For example, during the time of the Oakwood study, a companion study of literacy was conducted at an urban community college in Texas (Roueche and Comstock, 1981). We have reported some of the conclusions of that study in our final chapter since they buttress and illuminate our own judgments. We also know from the responses to presentations of this study made in national meetings, as well as from discussions with colleagues in many community colleges, that the conditions we report are widespread. We believe that the issues emphasized in this book exist in many colleges and deserve the careful consideration of all who share a concern for the relation between literacy and formal education.

To introduce our discussion of literacy at Oakwood College and place it in a broader perspective, this chapter presents a working definition of literacy and then considers the nature of literacy within a community college setting. Issues are raised concerning the impact of leveling down of college literacy standards on the student, the institution, and society.

Working Definition of Literacy

Following current trends, we view literacy as a functional and relational construct (Akinnaso, 1981; Whiteman, 1981). Literacy is not synonymous with reading and writing but requires consideration of the contexts in which written language is used as well as the goals that direct the reading and writing activity of particular individuals within those contexts. Contemporary literacy research includes efforts to discover how reading and writing fit into the ongoing activity of a particular context yet balances this focus with an emphasis on individuals and their goals. This dual approach avoids a view of the individual as a passive reactant, merely adapting behavior to the conventions of the setting. Although attention must certainly be paid to social norms, the reading and writing of individuals depend in part on the objectives for being in a given setting (Sticht, 1975). Individuals rarely engage in reading and writing as ends in themselves (Cole and Scribner, 1977). Almost always, reading and writing are embedded in activities linked to larger motives.

To capture its goal-directed, context-specific nature, we adopted a definition of literacy that draws on a transactional orientation (Meacham, 1975), systems theory (Bertalanffy, 1981), and a Soviet psychological theory of activity (Leont'ev, 1974, Vygotsky, 1962):

> Literacy is the use of reading and writing as *operations* in the service of a *goal* to accomplish *transactions* within a specific *context*.

This relational definition led us to identify qualitatively distinct varieties, or types, of literacy at Oakwood, defined in terms of changes in the subtle relationships among the goals, transactions, and contexts associated with reading and writing operations. Because literacy, considered in this way, proved to be a highly variable construct, we were precluded from making simple quantitative statements about high or low "levels" of literacy. However, the relational view aided our efforts to evaluate the literacy we observed in light of the overall goals and purposes of higher education.

Although we expected to find wide variation in specific reading and writing activities according to the characteristics of different classrooms, we reasoned that the requirements we observed, to be appropriate for college students, should emphasize *critical literacy*, as defined by two criteria. First, the requirements should be associated with well-articulated educational goals and, second, should involve high levels of independent thinking. Since these criteria were seldom met at Oakwood, our study documents the emphasis on a type of literacy having potentially negative consequences for the college and its students.

Understanding Literacy and Education

Historically, literacy has been considered a primary product of formal education, and literacy development has been included as a major objective of instructional activities at all levels. Individuals are expected to gain reading and writing skills commensurate with the level of formal education they receive. In fact, the reading abilities of individuals and the reading difficulty of materials have usually been expressed in terms of grade levels. In addition, academic uses of written language, especially those associated with college, have become the most socially valued forms of literacy. Literacy activities associated with scholarly endeavors, such as extensive and independent reading in multiple sources or the preparation of original essays, papers, and presentations, are accorded prestige in our society and are linked to the highest levels of learning. A college that encourages atypical uses of written language in contrast to these valued activities risks lowering its status and becoming less collegiate.

At the same time, however, colleges are expected to provide a relevant education, and suspicion is growing that academic literacy may be largely unrelated to functional literacy in other areas of life. Sociohistorical studies are challenging the notion that academic literacy is associated with economic prosperity and social mobility. Resnick and Resnick (1977, p. 371) note that "not all segments of the population have come to demand literacy skills of the kind that educators, members of Congress, and other government officials think necessary." Critics assert that secular "salvation" through literacy, like its earlier religious counterpart, has been promoted over the objections of people who see little real-world relevance in the literacy demands imposed on them in the educational setting.

Graff (1979) suggests that we have long been influenced by a literacy "myth." There is much evidence to suggest that we do not know what literacy means or what people should be expected to achieve as a result of higher literacy skills; and so we flail out at public schools for failing to accomplish the undefined while we apply, through the political process, standards that are inconsistent and contradictory.

Educational institutions are caught in a dilemma centering on the contemporary value of literacy. During the past few decades, public secondary and postsecondary institutions appear to have pursued relevance at the expense of concentrating on traditional forms of academic literacy. Community colleges, in particular, have attempted to respond to requests for services from all segments of the population. They have become the prototype of the open-access institution of higher education. Since the founding of the first public junior college in Joliet, Illinois, in 1901, they have been characterized by continuing expansion in terms of perceived mission and diversity of students served. With expansion have come shifts in the literacy emphasized.

The first mission, historically, involved offering the initial two years of the standard baccalaureate sequence. In paralleling university content and instructional techniques, the transfer function maintained the view that the literacy traditionally associated with higher education was intrinsically worthwhile. The transfer function remained the dominant purpose, as measured by student interests and numbers of faculty members involved, until the early seventies, when it was supplanted by vocational education as the first choice of a majority of students (Richardson and Leslie, 1980).

In vocational programs, traditional college literacy was downplayed in order to provide efficient, streamlined preparation in job-specific competencies. To make instruction accessible to as many students as possible, community colleges bypassed traditional forms of reading and writing by using alternative instructional techniques and technology.

The deemphasis on traditional college literacy has been extended by the growing importance of a third mission—continuing education, defined as enrollment in discrete courses without reference to programs or degrees. As early as 1976, a study of California community colleges concluded that continuing education for part-time adult students had become the dominant function (California Postsecondary Education Commission, 1981). The adult enrolled in a single course has become the modal community college student. The predominance of students less concerned with acquiring and developing the reading and writing skills associated with traditional degree programs has had a powerful impact in defining the norms for literacy on the campus.

Within the last decade, a developmental/remedial function has emerged. As Moore (1976) notes, the community college has taken on a "special commitment," a mission to serve those populations that had not previously found their way into the institution. Included in this group are students variously characterized as remedial, developmental, or underprepared because of their academic records and scores on standardized tests. These students arrive on campus in response to the institution's suggestion that they belong there, but often they are enrolled in special programs, peripheral to the regular curriculum and designed only to increase their proficiency in basic language skills. In effect, community colleges are taking on the responsibility for adult basic education (ABE), formerly the function of secondary schools operating through state-administered federal programs (Grede and Friedlander, 1981).

The developmental function of community colleges is becoming increasingly important as larger percentages of the student body lack the skills formerly associated with college course work. Developmental programs have proliferated in virtually all community colleges (Center for the Study of Community Colleges, 1978a, 1978b; Morrison and Ferrante, 1973; Roueche and Snow, 1977), but these delimited special programs do not begin to meet the needs for literacy skill development (Cohen, 1982). Because the developmental/remedial programs are unique in having a direct focus on reading and writing skills as a principal outcome, a paradox results on many campuses; a small number of peripheral courses in developmental studies continue to introduce students to academic forms of written language that are simultaneously being deemphasized in the rest of the college.

In response to changes in educational mission and student characteristics, community colleges have been decreasing the demands they place on students for forms of reading and writing traditionally associated with collegiate study. We contend that this change in the nature of college literacy has undesirable consequences for students and for society as a whole. A failure to address this issue must inevitably undermine public confidence in and support for open-access colleges as discussed below.

Literacy and College Students. Traditionally, collegiate programs have used written language as the vehicle to achieve the knowledge, cognitive skills, and attitudinal changes that are the desired outcomes of higher education (Brann, 1979). In particular, reading and writing have been associated with the development of thinking that is logical, explicit, abstract, and analytically powerful (Goody, 1977; Olson, 1977). Because of this association, a decline in the use of written language has been interpreted as a decline in cognitive potential. While the medium of instruction itself is not the crucial factor in determining the quality of educational outcomes (Akinnaso, 1981; Scollon and Scollon, 1981; Scribner and Cole, 1981), changes in media can be detrimental to learning if not accompanied by careful attention to consequences in terms of level and extensiveness of thinking and degree of independence of the learner.

For example, open-access colleges have been refining their occupational courses to impart essential technical content without requiring traditional forms of reading and writing. This change might have been applauded if the colleges had gone on to redefine forms of critical language use appropriate for the new technical learning. Because this has not been done, the result has been a decrease in opportunities to develop skill in critical thinking and independent expression.

At Oakwood, even though written language continued to be a primary medium of instruction, the level of thinking associated with reading and writing was quite low. Concurrently, the use of oral language and audiovisual media did not become any more critical or extensive. For these reasons, we could identify a trend in literacy that seemed to reduce the quality of instructional outcomes. To the extent that Oakwood students do not develop critical literacy skills, they and others like them will be less successful in meeting the cognitive and attitudinal demands of future education and employment, especially when competing with graduates of institutions where more rigorous literacy demands are imposed. College programs perform a disservice when their students, without essential cognitive and expressive skills, are not prepared to advance either in higher education or in the workplace (Yarrington, 1982).

Communication skills are becoming increasingly essential to employment even at entry levels, and the ability to process information independently and critically is vital to advancement. "Skills in reducing data, interpreting it, packaging it effectively, documenting decisions, explaining complex matter in simple terms, and persuading are highly prized in business, education, and the military and will become more so as the information explosion continues" (National Assessment of Educational Progress, 1981, p. 5). The fact that a few may be learning to become proficient in information use while the majority of the population becomes less able raises the specter of a two-class society of "those in control and those controlled" (Yarrington, 1982, p. 2). Open-access colleges like Oakwood may unwittingly be preparing students for slots in the lower strata of society from which they will not easily escape. In such circumstances, it is not surprising that educational credentials are becoming less of a gateway to social mobility. It is conceivable that employers will come to rely even less on the college degree to sort potential employees and will examine applicants with increasing emphasis on critical literacy skills.

Those who possess a college degree expect to receive preference for many types of employment over those who do not. They expect college credentials to be linked to occupational and social status as well as income. If this is no longer the case, attendance at community colleges will be increasingly less valuable to the individual.

Literacy and Society. Literacy has also been discussed in relation to the economic and social well-being of the larger society. Bormuth (1978), for example, has advanced the thesis that the gross national product is influenced by literacy. Increased literacy education has been seen as leading to increased productivity, relatively high standards of living, effective participation in democratic government, and advances in the arts and sciences (Eisenstein, 1980; Havelock, 1976). Public support for institutions of higher education rests on the assumption that the societal benefits accruing from investments in the education of individuals exceed the returns expected from alternative uses for the same funds.

This argument for public support is undercut significantly by reports of a lack of articulation between a community college education and effectiveness in the workplace, in the community, or in four-year colleges and universities. To the extent that degrees can be earned without developing the skills valued in society, the purpose of education shifts. Instead of being a societal investment, education becomes an individual consumption. The call for public subsidy can easily fall on deaf ears if college credentials do not guarantee exit competencies needed in employment and advanced education. If the public concludes that its educational programs no longer benefit individuals or society, community colleges will be in serious difficulty. Pragmatically, organizational survival dictates attention to the literacy issue.

Literacy and the Open-Access College

The evolutionary process of changing standards for literacy behaviors in higher education has affected all types of institutions. However, the procedures through which standards for literate behavior are identified and monitored seem to be disappearing more rapidly in open-access community colleges than in their more selective counterparts.

Clark (1960) discussed the impact of changing student objectives and characteristics on the community college's structure and curriculum. In Clark's words, "The mass enterprise in higher education contributes to a vast democratization, but it also entails a lowering of standards of admission and attainment" (p. 155). He defined the role of the community college as dealing with the potential dropout but added, "This perception has strong negative consequences for the status of the college in society" (p. 160).

London (1978) adds to concerns about quality with his graphic portrayal of current instructional processes in an urban community college in Massachusetts. On a typical day, more than half the student body was absent; busy students developed norms for regulating their efforts, budgeting time, and resisting teachers. Student resistance to the demands for critical literacy in the liberal arts courses led to a process of negotiation and ultimately to faculty modification of class demands in the face of a skeptical and unreceptive audience. A failure to modify classroom demands led, in one instance, to a student revolt. In a related study, Neumann and Riesman (1980) reported that students and faculty in community colleges were under pressure to conform to a set of norms at variance with activities traditionally regarded as prototypical of collegiate learning environments. Karabel (1972a, 1972b, 1974) suggested that community colleges perpetuate a class-based tracking system rather than promote social mobility because they do not emphasize higher-level language and thinking skills. There is increasing disjuncture between the skills developed through community college transfer programs and those demanded by four-year colleges and universities. The trend toward testing competencies as an alternative to accepting transcripts is one symptom of this developing gap.

Astin (1977) has suggested that high school graduates who initially attend four-year institutions are more likely to persist to a degree, as compared with those who initially attend two-year colleges, even when all major individual differences are taken into account. Olivas (1979) expressed concern about the implications of these conclusions for minorities, who are disproportionately concentrated in community colleges. Recently, Kissler (1980) and Kirst (1981) have noted the increasing proportion of community college transfers dropping out in academic difficulty from several University of California campuses. Kirst suggested that the trust needed to support the system in California was being eroded as students who entered underprepared as juniors experienced the problems of trying to catch up. In addition to concern for the transfer function, studies by Berg (1970), Wilms (1975, 1980), and Pincus (1980) have questioned the long-term economic payoff of vocational/technical programs to community college students. If credentials earned in open-access institutions are not reliable indicators of potential performance on the job or in the transfer classroom, the leveling up function of the entire postsecondary system is called into question. The apparent decline in the utility of a community college education has resulted, at least in part, from a failure to emphasize the development of critical literacy skills—especially at a time when technological developments in the larger society widen the gulf between those who are and those who are not critically literate. The negative consequences of a long-term decline in critical literacy seem sufficiently serious to merit public concern.

As a leader in promoting open access to higher education, the community college has clearly contributed to the changing standards for literacy. Our purpose in writing this book, however, is not to criticize open-access institutions for effectively pursuing societal aspirations that in retrospect appear to have had detrimental, as well as favorable, consequences. Rather, we believe that examination of current practice reveals alternatives through which current trends can be reversed. A major purpose in sharing the results of our research is to encourage open-access institutions to experiment with practices through which they can transform themselves from a part of the problem to a part of the solution.

Organization of the Book

In keeping with our definition of literacy, our case study at Oakwood includes descriptions of the campus *contexts* for literacy and how they were established, the *goals* toward which reading and writing were directed, and the *activities* (transactions) within which they were enacted, as well as the written language *operations* themselves. To document the lack of critical literacy, we discuss the evidence we found that reading and writing were not associated with well-articulated educational goals and did not involve high levels of independent thought.

Chapter Two provides an overview of Oakwood College, its history, and its current situation with regard to mission, curriculum, students, faculty, and administration. Chapters Three and Four describe specific classroom settings and analyze reading and writing in these settings. To bring out the goal-directed aspect of literacy, Chapters Five and Six, respectively, discuss the objectives of instructors and the motives of students. Chapter Seven focuses on the nonclassroom campus and the relationship to literacy of certain administrative tasks and student support services. Chapter Eight considers administrative priorities and strategies to show how they influence faculty commitment and, through faculty, critical literacy. Chapter Nine analyzes how critical literacy can be promoted within the organizational context of open-access colleges.

CHAPTER TWO

❧ ❧ ❧

The College Setting

❧ ❧ ❧

We begin our account of literacy at Oakwood with an overview of the college and the Richfield District. Such an introduction to the institution provides essential background for the detailed information about literacy to be presented in later chapters. Because we view literacy as a fluctuating, situation-specific phenomenon, we need to put it into context before we can understand it. The following descriptions of curriculum, administration, faculty, and students illustrate the complex, dynamic character of this community college as the setting for a study of literacy.

At the same time, this portrait of Oakwood College and the Richfield District emphasizes the relevance of our findings about college literacy. Oakwood is not unique; rather, in its clientele, programs, practices, and priorities, it is typical of open-door community colleges. In fact, Oakwood is representative of the best of its type, and it functions within a competently managed district. The observations about literacy at Oakwood reported in this volume could probably be duplicated in most community colleges.

Richfield District

Richfield District was established in 1962 as a result of a popular election following enabling state legislation. The district was a descendant of the original community/junior college movement, developing from the same roots that had given rise to Joliet Junior College in 1901. From its inception, Richfield assumed responsibility for the preexisting college, which had been administered by a local high school district. To improve service to the expanding population of the district, extension centers were created under the administration of the original college. The subsequent growth of these centers prompted the establishment, in 1965, of two new independent colleges, one of which became Oakwood.

In 1968 a fourth college was added to offer a large selection of occupational and technical programs. This event marked the emergence of occupational/technical education as a major function of the district. During the 1970s, the district continued to grow, adding one other comprehensive college. In 1978 the board approved the establishment of a sixth college. This nontraditional "college without walls," serving the entire district, met with great opposition from faculty members and many college administrators. A final traditional college, geographically situated to serve the district's large Hispanic population, opened its door in the fall of 1980.

During little more than fifteen years, Richfield grew from a single college enrolling 8,900 students to a seven-college district enrolling almost 60,000 students in credit programs. By 1980-81 Richfield employed some 1,500 full-time staff members, including 740 instructors and 220 administrators; the remainder worked in such areas as office support, maintenance, and food services. In addition, the district employed a large and growing number of part-time faculty members, as has been the trend among institutions of its type.

In 1970 the state system to which Richfield belonged established a funding formula such that the state paid half the operating costs, the other half being distributed between local taxes and the federal government. Students paid fees to support noninstructional activities, but the institutions were tuition-free. The allocation of state funds was based on a formula using full-time student equivalents, which encouraged districts to expand enrollments as a way of increasing revenues. Until 1978 Richfield used this strategy as a way of keeping ahead of inflation. In that year, requests exceeded state appropriations, which by then had declined to about 27 percent of Richfield's operational budget. The following year, the state legislature, in anticipation of a "Proposition 13" initiative, passed a law limiting increases in the district property tax, which had been forced to assume an ever-increasing share of the burden of financing district growth. By 1979–80 Richfield District was feeling the same fiscal pinch as its counterparts across the country as it struggled to cope with inflation, increased costs for maintenance and utilities, and higher salaries and fringe benefits for a highly tenured faculty. Contributing to the fiscal problem was the absence of increased state dollars to offset the limitation on local taxing authority. Tuition was imposed for the first time in the history of the district.

Governance. The Richfield District was governed by an elected lay board with taxing authority within the limitations imposed by the state legislature. The local board was, in turn, responsible to a state board appointed by the governor and having general responsibility for overseeing the state's system of community colleges. Although the existence of two governing boards sounds unwieldy, in practice this arrangement functioned very well. The local board maintained a service-area orientation, while the state board satisfied concerns of the governor and legislature for accountability. Because state board members were frequently appointed from the ranks of former local board members, for the most part the boards understood and respected each other.

The local board employed a chief executive with the title of chancellor. The chancellor, in turn, relied on two groups of executives as his principal agents: three vice-chancellors and seven college presidents. Before the arrival of the new chancellor who took office in 1977, the district had operated from a single-college model, with the chief executive titled "president" and the heads of the various campuses termed "executive deans."

During the growth of the early and middle seventies, governance for the Richfield District was highly centralized, with all major decisions made at the top. It was common for governing board members to intervene in administrative decisions, and the district had at one time been under sanctions from its regional accrediting association to bring the problem under control. Governing board involvement resulted in an oppressive political climate and low administrative morale.

Interestingly, the centralization of decision making and extensive board involvement did not imply control of the educational program. Negotiations between faculty and district administrators had produced an extensive codification of policies for the residential faculty, effectively insulating it and most of the curriculum from the machinations at the district level. Although the policies were useful in keeping education and politics separate until the arrival of the new chancellor, their existence posed an additional obstacle to change when the district climate had stabilized and administrators were able to turn their attention to issues related to the curriculum.

District Administration. It is hard to imagine a better setting for examining the potential influence of administrative behavior on literacy in educational programs and services than the circumstances that existed in February 1979. A new, competent, and nationally respected team of leaders was in the final stages of stabilizing relationships between the governing board and the college district. To formalize this development, the chancellor had drawn a "code of ethics" designed to formalize board/district interaction. The document outlined legal powers, responsibilities, and ethical obligations. Accepted by the board in early 1978, the code read, in part: "The board asserts its responsibilities [to] urge all employees to avail themselves of all administrative remedies and procedures before requesting governing board involvement." Having established a solid working relationship with the board, the new team prepared to turn its attention to changes it perceived necessary to bring the district into the leadership ranks of large community college districts.

The district office was geographically separated from the seven colleges whose activities it coordinated. Although each college had its own administrative staff, nearly 40 percent of the administrators in the district were located in the district office. Structurally, the district office was divided into three major functional areas, as shown in Figure 1.

An executive vice-chancellor was responsible for business and fiscal functions, facilities planning, and computer services. Of the three major functional areas, this was the most highly centralized and hierarchally structured. The executive vice-chancellor was the only one of the four top district officers who had served in the previous administration, and so his experience and preferences related to a more centralized form of operation than that initiated by the new chancellor. Despite this difference, the two worked well together.

The vice-chancellor for educational development played a central role in bringing about changes in the educational program. His responsibilities included coordinating instructional services, curriculum development, educational planning, student services, institutional studies, staff development, and a wide range of other activities. Among the senior administrators, he served as the principal change agent. His staff was highly decentralized. Interactions were informal, all staff members having direct access to him.

The team was rounded out by a vice-chancellor for employee relations whose responsibilities included personnel, affirmative action, and employee negotiations. Although the district was not formally organized for collective bargaining, by tradition a meet-and-confer process had been used for establishing policies on compensation and working conditions. Over time, a very extensive codification of the agreements growing out of this process had developed, which the faculty viewed as its contract with the board. The accumulated faculty policies formed a major obstacle to change. They also became the focus of considerable conflict when the board made a take-it-or-leave-it offer for a salary increase during the first year of the study.

Figure 1. Organizational Chart for Richfield District, 1979–80.

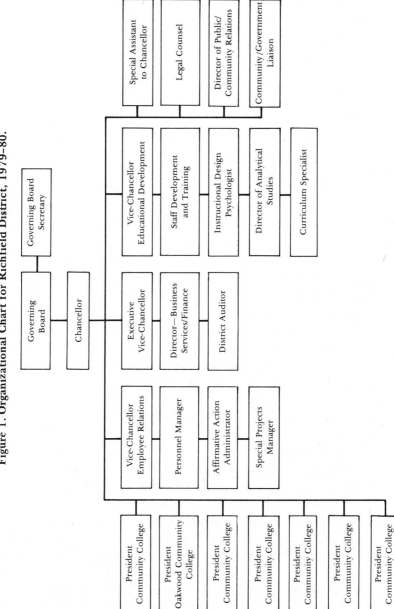

The resulting turmoil, as well as the jockeying for position of two organizations competing to represent the faculty, made the vice-chancellor for employee relations a key element in the district's change strategy. In degree of centralization and hierarchal structure, this office fell somewhere between the extremes represented by the two other vice-chancellors.

During most of the study, there existed a chancellor's executive council comprising the four senior district officers and the seven college presidents. In the second year of the study, the president of the faculty executive council was added. This body served as the central forum for establishing district policies and direction. Late in the study, somewhat to the presidents' consternation, the chancellor withdrew from the group, delegating responsibilities of the chair to the vice-chancellor for educational development. Aiding the council in its coordinating and planning responsibilities were twenty-eight districtwide committees, representative of the seven colleges and the district office, and ranging from "athletics" to "energy use." As a major college within a highly centralized multicampus district, Oakwood was strongly affected by the activities and priorities of the central administration. However, it maintained its own identity consistent with the characteristics of its students, faculty, administrative history, and evolving curriculum.

Oakwood College

To the extent that it is meaningful to characterize any community college as typical, Oakwood merited that description. Founded in the middle sixties, when such institutions were being established at the rate of one a week, Oakwood offered the comprehensive curriculum that normally accompanies the open-door philosophy. Although Oakwood exhibited unique properties related to its history as part of the Richfield District, in changing student clientele, fiscal constraints, and use of adjunct faculty it greatly resembled other community colleges that are part of urban, multicampus districts.

In 1966–67 Oakwood had enrolled 4,000 students, yielding a full-time equivalency of 2,700. Ten years later, the comparable figures were 12,000 and 7,000. Most community colleges like Oakwood are funded on the basis of their full-time equivalent enrollments. For its entire history, Oakwood had been accustomed to offsetting losses due to inflation by increasing enrollments more rapidly than costs. By 1978, however, Oakwood had to adapt its educational program and services in the face of declining numbers of full-time students interested in the transfer programs and greater student diversity among those recruited to offset the loss in traditional enrollments. Although enrollments continued to increase, significantly larger proportions of the new students were part-time. More attended in the evening; and increasingly, those in attendance lacked the writing, reading, and math skills regarded by the faculty as minimal for success in the transfer programs.

The use of adjunct faculty had played an important role in Oakwood's development. In 1966–67 there was one full-time faculty member for every twenty-eight full-time student equivalents. By 1978 the ratio was one to forty-three, excluding counselors and library staff. The use of adjunct faculty in the day program was condemned by full-time faculty members, but there was no similar complaint about the evening program, because full-time faculty members were given preference for evening assignments and received extra compensation for accepting them.

Curriculum. The purposes and goals of an institution are reflected in its curriculum. Any analysis of the role played by literacy within instructional activity must begin with a description of the programmatic structure through which administrators, faculty members, and students meld institutional purposes and their own value preferences. The curriculum at Oakwood was a logical extension of the mission and educational priorities of the Richfield District. Course offerings were comprehensive, within allowances made for an administrative decision of the late sixties to concentrate technical programs requiring heavy capital investment on a campus strategically located to serve the entire metropolitan area. Oakwood also followed national trends in the nature of its curriculum, which was increasing in comprehensiveness but decreasing in coherence and structure.

Curriculum may be defined as the courses and patterns of courses offered by the institution in order to present the knowledge, principles, values, and skills that are the intended consequences of instructional activity (Carnegie Foundation for the Advancement of Teaching, 1977). At Oakwood, the curriculum was organized in four major categories:

• *Transfer education*—an academic program comparable to the freshman and sophomore years at state universities.

• *Occupational education*—programs emphasizing job-ready training to minimize the completion time required and maximize skill development to meet job-market demands.

• *Developmental education*—training in basic skills for adults to help them function in complex society and/or prepare them for entry into college-level occupational or academic programs. Its specific objectives were to improve skills in communication (listening, speaking, reading, writing), computation, human relations, decision-making skills, and study skills.

• *Continuing education*—opportunities for citizens of the community to enrich their lives as wage earners, as members of the society, and as residents of the world of leisure. These opportunities were provided through all the educational programs as well as through noncredit courses, seminars, lectures, workshops, and other educational and cultural activities.

All four major functional areas of instruction had been part of the Oakwood curriculum since its founding. The priorities accorded these program areas resulted from changing internal and external influences. At Oakwood's inception, its commitment was predominantly to transfer education; its rhetoric at that time clearly had the flavor of a liberal arts tradition. In its catalogue, the college described its overall function as "the education of the whole man" and elaborated a "three-point program to accomplish this purpose: (1) to help the development of individuals seeking maturity of mind and body; (2) to transmit to interested persons the accumulated wealth of our culture and traditions; and (3) to assist nonmatriculating students to update their knowledge and skills for a better adjustment to a changing world."

Over the years, an increasing share of the college's curriculum was devoted to occupational education. The 1970s saw the establishment of fourteen occupational degree programs and six certificate offerings. At the time our study ended, an additional twelve career programs or options were pending. During the seventies, Oakwood experienced the same change in student preferences from transfer to occupational programs observed in similar institutions across the country. Current enrollment and funding patterns suggested no diminution in the growth of this occupational component.

Most recently, the college had indicated its intention to address the needs of new and nontraditional students as defined by Cross (1976) by allocating funds for "developmental education." Developmental education also expanded during the 1970s, and by 1979 Oakwood offered fifty-three sections enrolling 1,240 students. Over 15 percent of day students and 7 percent of evening students were enrolled in developmental courses. More than three fourths of these were high school graduates, and 22 percent were Mexican-American, almost twice the percentage of that group in the total student population.

The changes in the developmental area were not confined to growth. From its inception, Oakwood offered developmental courses with a remedial focus, as suggested by an early issue of the college catalogue: ". . . develop basic skills in fundamental areas to enhance the ability to succeed in more rigorous academic and career programs." However, a new program was instituted in 1978, the adult basic skills program, which reflected a different conception of developmental education. This program, offered in two twelve-hour blocks, included special courses in reading, math, counseling, and English. Students were placed in these blocks on the basis of test results. Also offered as part of the basic skills program was intensive English for Spanish speakers, designed for students who had not developed reading and writing skills either in their native tongue or in English.

In the following year, a Developmental Education Task Force for the Richfield District, strongly influenced by the basic skills blocks at Oakwood, developed a new statement of purpose for the report of the District Council on Educational Priorities. The new statement read as follows: "The purpose of the developmental studies program is to prepare the citizen to better function in the larger society by strengthening basic societal skills. The return on this investment is an individual better able to seek employment, to further [his or her] education, and to be a successful taxpayer."

Several aspects of this statement deserve special attention. First, as stated elsewhere in the report, the intent was clearly to address "new" clients without strong academic skills and "underprepared" for traditional college work. Second, the report clearly turned away from the remedial emphasis to focus on a broader definition of *developmental,* encompassing, in the words of Cross (1976, p. 31), "the diverse talents of students, whether academic or not." The purpose of developmental education, according to the new definition included in the report of the district advisory committee, was to focus on assisting students to achieve their goals—"to take students from where they are to where they want to go." This would be accomplished by providing both academic and nonacademic "human" skills.

The task force seemed to be moving toward a goal of functional literacy, with less, rather than more, emphasis on the traditional aspects of academic literacy. This difference was not lost on many faculty members, who maintained an ambivalence toward the new programs. On the one hand, they saw advantages in the form of the removal of students they regarded as unqualified from their own classes. On the other, they were concerned about the impact on the credibility of other college offerings, as well as the possibility that the new program would compete for scarce resources once district discretionary dollars had been exhausted.

The 1979–81 Oakwood catalogue listed 760 courses from the district course bank. Courses were listed at three academic levels: the "sub-100," or "developmental," level; the "100," or "introductory," level; and the "200," or "advanced," level. These courses were subsumed under transfer, occupational, and developmental categories. The decision to place a course in one of these categories was at least as much a fiscal as an educational decision. Transfer and developmental education were funded at a base level, while courses qualifying for the coveted occupational classification received additional funding from the state. Courses offered for continuing education without credit received no state reimbursement. The practice was to designate as occupational any course that could meet the state board review criteria. Whenever possible, noncredit continuing education offerings were also "upgraded" to credit status. Breneman and Nelson (1981) have reported the prevalence of similar practices among community colleges nationwide as one response to growing financial constraints.

A variety of terms were used in Oakwood publications to refer to the patterns of courses that made up the curriculum. The terminology was not always used consistently. The college's rapid growth, both in expansion of educational goals and in the increase in numbers of students, had produced few opportunities for consolidation or refinement of institutional procedures. Thus, curriculum at Oakwood might refer to any of the following:

• A prescribed series of courses required to earn the associate in applied science (A.A.S.) degree in a particular occupational area—for example, electronics technology. These *programs* were designed to take the full-time student two years to complete. They included a districtwide general education requirement.

• A somewhat more flexible series of courses that a student might follow to earn an associate of arts (A.A.) degree or to transfer to a four-year college to pursue the baccalaureate degree. These were also called *advisement packages.* Some advisement packages closely resembled the first two years of course work in the related area at the state university. Others, such as ethnic studies, had no parallel. Students were permitted to combine an advisement package with general education requirements to obtain an A.A. or an associate in general studies (A.G.S.) degree.

• A prescribed series of courses in a particular occupational area—for example, automotive chassis—required to earn a *certificate.* The career-specific courses were the same as those required for the A.A.S. However, certificate programs generally required no general education courses and could be completed in a year or less by a full-time student.

• A *sequence* represented an institutional decision that courses within a particular department or group of related departments had to be taken in a specified order. Sequences were discouraged unless required (as in math and science), because of the impact on enrollments in the more advanced courses and the corresponding possibility that such courses would not be offered because of low enrollments.

• A *block* was a planned series of self-contained courses designed to assist adults in the development of reading, mathematics, and English skills. Even though the courses in a block were clearly remedial, the institution allowed a maximum of 12 credits from such courses toward the A.G.S. degree in order to preserve student eligibility for federal financial assistance.

• A student was also able to follow none of the institutionally developed patterns of courses but, rather, design an individualized pattern. These *idiosyncratic patterns* could also be combined with general education requirements to earn the A.A. or A.G.S. degree. Figure 2 summarizes the patterns that made up the curriculum at Oakwood.

Official district and college documents seemed to indicate that considerable attention had been devoted to developing coherent programs of study for students. However, the elaborate structuring of the curriculum did not translate into measurable results. Despite the impressive enrollment figures, relatively few students graduated (less than 5 percent of the head count and 10 percent of the full-time equivalents), an experience common to most open-access institutions of this type. Students transferring to four-year institutions typically did so without completing an A.A. degree, and students in occupational courses often found and took jobs before completing an A.A.S. program.

One reason for the low completion rate was, of course, the large numbers of part-time students. Like their counterparts in community colleges elsewhere, Oakwood administrators explained the low completion rate as a result of students' attending for reasons other than degree attainment. The assumption accompanying this rationale was that students were achieving their objectives to a satisfactory extent even though such objectives were largely undefined and the level of achievement un-

Figure 2. Course Patterns at Oakwood Community College.

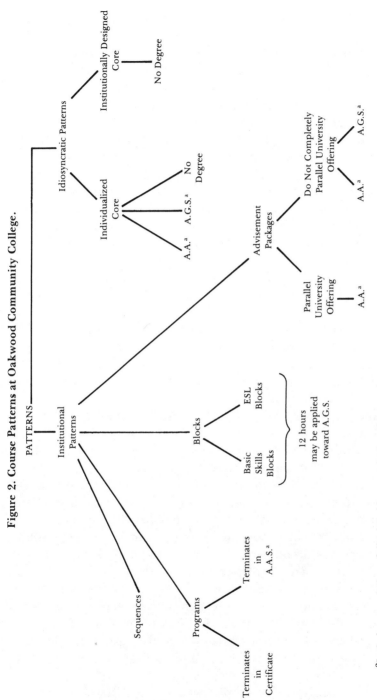

[a]Includes completion of districtwide general education requirements.

measured. It is an unstated corollary of community college philosophy that questioning the benefits of attendance constitutes heresy.

Nonetheless, the institution invested little effort in developing effective advising for students and did little to facilitate an optimal structuring of course experiences. For example, even a simple sequencing of courses was not maintained, because official course prerequisites were seldom enforced. Most programs of study were administered, at least nominally, by departments, which were responsible for designing and updating the patterns and maintaining records of students using them. However, the extent to which departments actually exercised this function was quite variable and, overall, minimal. By 1980 the typical student at Oakwood did not complete any program of instruction but left after taking one or more individual courses.

Administration. As noted previously, the Richfield District had traditionally operated with a strongly centralized administration. Until the new chancellor took office in 1977, the chief administrator at Oakwood held the title of executive dean. Areas such as food service, maintenance of buildings and grounds, security, bookstore, and fiscal services were all controlled by a vice-president in the district office.

During the period of the study, a decision was made to decentralize responsibilities for a number of these functions, and the title of the campus chief executive officer was changed to *president*. Oakwood administrators viewed with mixed emotions the decision to decentralize. They liked the idea of greater autonomy, but they were concerned that increased responsibilities were not accompanied by increases in administrative staff for the college. To complicate matters further, some key college-based personnel, including the fiscal officer and the managers of food service and the bookstore, continued to report to a district officer. Of most concern was the divided allegiance of the fiscal officers, who, in the words of one administrator, "for a $17,000 salary were supposed to keep both college- and district-level officers happy and out of trouble."

As part of the decentralization effort, district officers had encouraged presidents to establish "management teams."At Oakwood the team included, in addition to the president, two deans (instruction and student services), three associate deans (admissions and records, continuing and special education, occupational education), and three directors (evaluation and research, student activities, special services). Significantly, administrators reporting to district officers were excluded from the team by design, resulting in communication problems as well as increased coordinating responsibilities for members of the team. Figures 3 and 4 provide additional information about the Oakwood administrative structure during the period of the study.

The administrative council met weekly and served as the coordinating structure for the management team. Meetings were informal, did not involve agendas or minutes, and served mainly to facilitate communication. Frequently, the president or other team members reported on meetings they had attended. Much less frequently, one member would present a problem to the council, and discussion involving the entire group would follow. Decisions were rarely reached in these sessions. The president listened carefully to everything that was said and then made his own decision, which might or might not coincide with the advice he had received. Sometimes the council was used to define the college's official position on an issue being considered by the district. Defining an official position was important because of the variety of district meetings attended by the different council members where the issue might be discussed. Finally, the council also provided a source of mutual support for its members in times of stress.

Next to the administrative council, the most important committee meeting at Oakwood involved department chairs and was conducted by the dean of instruction. Such meetings were held three or four times each semester in accordance with a published schedule. Often in attendance, but not as very active participants, were the dean of student services and associate deans whose areas of responsibility corresponded to items under discussion. The meeting of department chairs served primarily coordinating and problem-solving functions. Because department chairs had faculty status, these meetings repre-

Figure 3. Staffing Chart for Oakwood Community College, 1979-80.

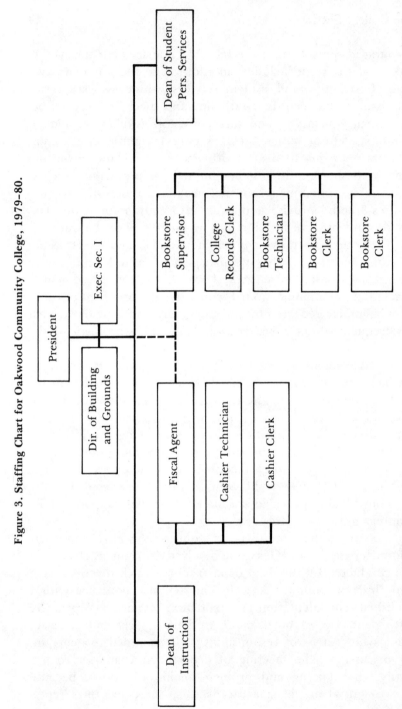

Note: Dashed line indicates staff relationship. These positions reported to the executive vice-chancellor through the line organization.

Figure 4. Details of Organizational Structure: Office of Instruction and Office Student Personnel Services.

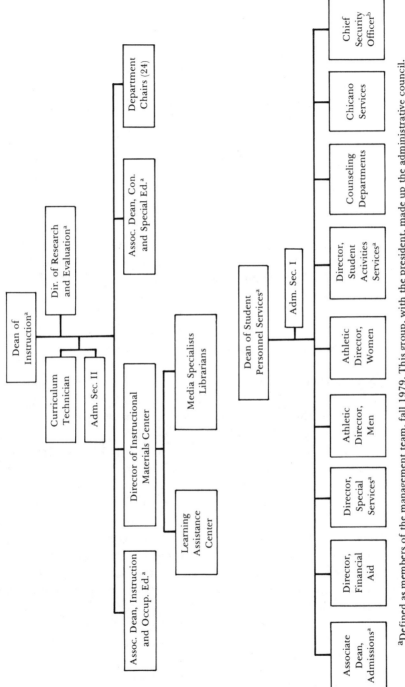

[a]Defined as members of the management team, fall 1979. This group, with the president, made up the administrative council.
[b]This position became a campus, as distinct from a district, responsibility during the study.

sented one important interface between administrative and faculty priorities and values.

Department chairs were selected for rotating terms by the faculties of their departments, subject to approval by the president. The 182 full-time faculty members were distributed among twenty-six departments ranging in size from two or three members to twenty-seven. Counseling, which reported to the dean of students, and the instructional materials center both held status as departments. Chairs did not receive released time unless there were at least nine members in the department, and so the time available to them for administration, given the fifteen-hour teaching load, was quite limited. As a result of prior negotiations between the faculty association and the district, additional compensation for chairs had been stressed at the expense of released time. In one department with 27.5 full-time equivalent faculty members in the day program, the chair taught twelve hours one semester and nine hours the other. In addition, she had general responsibilities for an evening program that was about one third as large as the day program. A number of chairs taught extra courses in the evening for extra compensation. There was one chair who received no released time, because his department was too small, but who taught extra courses in the evening and carried on a private business on the side.

Partly as a result of the imposing time commitments of chairs, the departments made few demands on instructors beyond course scheduling and text selection. There were rarely more than two meetings during an academic year, and these were held mainly to disseminate information. Class responsibilities were often structured in a relatively informal way during department meetings as chairs discussed class and time preferences with instructors. Departments did not appear to take the initiative with respect to either curricular or instructional adaptation.

In addition to the department structure, there were twenty-one college committees, the most important of which was the one on curriculum. Most had an average of five members, with one or two inactive. Administrators typically served as committee chairs or as ex officio members. The more important committees, such as curriculum, often had several administrators in attendance. Committee work was one of the demands placed on instructors both by the administration and by other instructors. The most active committee during 1979-80 was the one on advisement and registration, which met weekly and did an enormous amount of work in producing an adviser's handbook and reorganizing the advising and registration process. At the opposite end of the spectrum were several committees that met rarely and accomplished little that was visible.

During the study, three full-time faculty members served in quasi-administrative roles to provide faculty leadership and administrative support for staff development activities, the developmental studies task force, and the advisement and registration committee. Each of these areas was critical to the plans of the dean of instruction for achieving directed change. These faculty members were selected because of their commitment to serving students with limited reading and writing skills, an important administrative priority. They were given released time or summer employment through use of discretionary funds provided by the district, augmented by college funds where necessary.

The role of quasi-administrators was ambiguous. They were asked to perform administrative tasks but were not given administrative support services such as secretarial help, access to duplicating services, or telephones in their offices where these were not already available. They were not invited to administrative meetings and lacked authority to implement any of the recommendations growing out of their activities. Administrators did not view them as performing administrative roles, while other faculty members sometimes resented the contributions these quasi-administrators made to achieving change desired by district administrators. Because all three of the quasi-administrators were women, they attributed many of the less desirable aspects of their role to their sex, with some justification. One commented, "The men were less willing to do it because they have been here so long. . . . Women will work much harder because they have not reached their level of incompetency."

Faculty. The full-time faculty at Oakwood was predominantly male (65 percent), experienced, and heavily tenured. In 1976–77, just before being visited for reaccreditation, Oakwood had added twenty-two new faculty members. During the following three years, the greatest number of new hires in any year was three. As the fourth contract was a tenure appointment, few faculty members had a provisional status at the time of our study.

Most of the transfer-oriented departments had higher percentages of full-time resident faculty members than their shares of the enrollment justified. Part of the imbalance resulted from the practice of staffing full-time faculty members at 90 percent of the day enrollment only. All evening classes were taught by part-time faculty or by full-time faculty members who voluntarily accepted an overload for which they were reimbursed at the part-time rate. Evening enrollments had been increasing more rapidly than day enrollments, so the ratio of full-time resident faculty members to total full-time student equivalents (FTSE) had therefore steadily declined. More than half of all instruction was offered by staff members on adjunct appointments. The adjunct staff numbered 300 in the evening and 72 during the day, in comparison with 163 full-time teaching faculty members.

The transfer orientation of the Oakwood faculty was evident in the numbers that possessed the doctorate. Thirty-five—more than 21 percent—held this degree, a high percentage by community college standards. By 1979 Oakwood had about one fourth of its full-time student equivalents enrolled in occupational courses. Reflecting the fact that much of the demand for occupational offerings was in the evening, only about one fifth of the resident faculty had occupational specializations. The difference between student orientations and preparation of resident faculty members was even more striking when nursing was excluded. The nursing department, because of state requirements, had 21 percent of the resident faculty assigned to occupational areas but generated less than 10 percent of the occupational FTSE.

There were few minority-group members among the full-time faculty, a situation that produced stress as the minority student population, particularly Hispanics, continued to increase more rapidly than the college's total enrollment.

The regular teaching load was thirty to thirty-two hours per year, calculated according to a complex formula involving type of contact and class size. In addition to teaching responsibilities, faculty members were expected to fulfill thirty hours of accountability per week, including one scheduled office hour each day. Since arrangements for monitoring accountability were nonexistent, some instructors paid little attention to the policy, including the keeping of scheduled office hours. Beyond regular loads, faculty members were permitted to teach an additional nine load hours for extra pay during the academic year and six load hours during the summer. A significant number took advantage of this opportunity to increase incomes.

Faculty members also received extra pay for such activities as coordination of co-op work experience or the foreign study series, substitute teaching, supervision of the evening program, summer work other than teaching, nonclassroom instructional activities, course management, and coaching. The arrangements for extra compensation were quite comprehensive. The typical attitude of a faculty member at Oakwood was that if an out-of-class responsibility was not spelled out in the policies or if arrangements were not made for extra compensation, the activity did not need to be undertaken.

Faculty members at Oakwood were well paid and enjoyed good fringe benefits. They were allowed to advance on the salary schedule for travel; attendance at clinics, conferences, and workshops; work experience; and taking additional course work. The policy was particularly advantageous to instructors in occupational areas such as electronics and data processing, who were able to work summers at a higher rate of pay in industry and receive credit on the salary scale as well. The highest paid faculty member at Oakwood during 1979–80 earned more than $40,000.

Perhaps 15 percent of faculty members conducted outside businesses. The flexible arrangements on accountability encouraged this type of activity. Opportunities for earning extra compensation made it difficult to recruit and retain administrators from the ranks of the faculty. The option of returning to the faculty possessed by most Oakwood administrators was frequently exercised, resulting in a high turnover rate among campus administrators below the level of president.

The most important faculty organization in the Richfield District was the faculty association. Historically, this group had represented the faculty in governance issues and had conducted districtwide negotiations for salaries and working conditions. In negotiations, the association functioned as a de facto union.

Students. Like many community colleges, Oakwood found the demographics of its student body undergoing significant change. In the late seventies, students were characterized by an increasing diversification of objectives, interests, ethnic backgrounds, and abilities. Blacks and Chicanos formed about 15 percent of the student population at Oakwood. Both minority groups were internally cohesive, although the Chicanos were the more visible in terms of numbers and political activity. In comparison to the student body of the sixties, the median age was older, more attended part-time, an increasing percentage were women, and educational objectives focused most frequently on the vocational offerings. By the time this study began, 70 percent of the student body attended part-time, and the modal student was an older female, taking one course and not interested in completing a degree.

Of greater import, Oakwood, a college firmly rooted in the academic tradition and committed to baccalaureate-oriented courses as its first priority, was faced with a growing number of poorly prepared students. Instructors reported significant changes in students during the previous five or six years. Skill levels, motivation, and attitudes were mentioned. Students were perceived as poor readers and writers, and their lack of motivation and seriousness made it harder for faculty members to derive satisfaction from teaching.

Instructors noted changes over the years in the classroom behavior of students: They appeared to be less mature, with the concomitant problems of short attention spans and poor-quality work. Specific examples of changes in students' behavior included not checking their own work, not asking questions if they did not understand, and not wanting explanations for information. This was particularly true of some of the younger students entering Oakwood right out of high school. As a faculty member commented:

> These students are so ill prepared for college that they think they want to learn but are not willing to undergo the torment of learning because there is a certain amount of aggravation with learning. When you're learning, it's stress. It should be pleasurable—let's hope it's pleasurable—but there has to be some stress because you are making an effort to learn something that you didn't know before. I think that they think a junior college is going to be just a glorified high school, it's going to be an easy breeze.

An instructor observed the grade-oriented nature of current students:

> The kids will argue with you on points that they never would have even remotely thought worth mentioning, because they are so concerned about the grade rather than what they are learning. This is very marked in the classes, very marked.

Changing classroom behavior was related to identified changes in student goals. Instructors noted that students seemed less interested and often were not working toward achieving specific goals.

A minority opinion on ability and basic skills suggested that although students were more diverse, on the average they were equivalent to previous students. The majority of instructors, however, identified specific changes in their students' basic skills. Reading was seen as more of a problem than ten years earlier. "It makes no difference how easy the book is, some students still can't read it."

In most classes, writing was also a major problem. Even in an occupational course that did not include writing requirements, the instructor was concerned about the amount of time she had to spend teaching basic grammar and spelling skills. One transfer instructor stated, "Writing skills have deteriorated." Another commented, "It is hard to figure out what the student is trying to say. . . . There is a worsening ability to express even simple ideas." Some instructors noted that the increase in writing problems was the chief reason they had moved from essay to objective exams.

Instructors whose courses included even a small amount of mathematics stated that it was necessary to spend more time teaching basic math or algebra. In occupational courses, it was noted that students had a terrible time even adding numbers. In two higher-level transfer courses, the instructor noted that he spent time teaching basic algebra and trying to eliminate fears of mathematics. Another stated, "Most students have poor math backgrounds. . . . The primary and secondary educational system is failing to produce literate people."

Vocabulary and listening had also declined, according to some instructors. One commented, "Students coming right out of high school have poor vocabularies." Another put it this way: "Reading comprehension gives them the most problems, followed by listening skills." Instructors were also concerned with thinking skills. One noted, "The greatest discrepancy between what is real and what is ideal for my students is an ability to draw logical conclusions."

In contrast, faculty members generally endorsed the increase in older returning students. They felt that older students had better skills, particularly grammar skills and listening skills. Also important, such students had a more mature outlook on life and more experience with the world. Consequently, they were often more inclined to participate in class discussions and to see the relevance of material presented. As one faculty member noted, "The older student is a better listener and generally a better student and more motivated."

Still, the overall perception of changes in the student population was not positive. In summarizing the situation, a faculty member stated, "Overall, students have not learned to think, to read, to spell, or to add and subtract." Another speculated that probably the skill level had gone down because the college encouraged greater numbers of students to attend. However, he acknowledged, "It is also possible that the passage of time makes you think back to 'the good old days.' "

Summary Discussion

This chapter has introduced Oakwood College and the Richfield District in order to establish the context within which our study of literacy and its correlates was conducted. Although we make no claims that Oakwood was representative of all open-door community colleges, it is useful to summarize Oakwood's similarities to other colleges and its unique characteristics.

The Richfield District and Oakwood College, like the majority of urban multicampus community colleges, were established in the early to middle sixties. Initially, emphasis was placed on university parallel programs to provide students with an opportunity to complete the first two years of a baccalaureate degree before transferring to a four-year institution. Unlike many community colleges in California and other Western states, Richfield District continued a strong emphasis on transfer as the primary function past the middle of the 1970s. Recent studies had revealed stronger-than-national-average performance, persistence, and degree attainment for transfer students from the district's colleges at the state universities.

Rapid growth in numbers of students and in numbers of colleges characterized the district until the early 1980s, when alternating years of decline and growth indicate stabilization or a much more modest growth rate than in the past. Interestingly, the year of most significant decline followed hard on the heels of the district's most aggressive marketing campaign, conducted according to all the best thinking on this subject. In retrospect, it now appears that the efforts of the district's new administrative leadership in emphasizing continuing education, alternative delivery methods, and career education and in recruiting nontraditional clients postponed, but did not prevent, the necessity of coming to grips with a declining potential student population.

Combined with reductions in the growth rate have been the same changes in student-body demographics reported by virtually all open-door colleges. Students are older and more likely to represent racial or ethnic minorities. They are less interested in earning degrees, enroll in fewer courses, and are described as having reduced competencies in reading, writing, and mathematics.

The tendency for more students to attend part-time, to be less interested in earning degrees, and to possess lower skill levels has important implications for the financial well-being of institutions such as Oakwood, which are funded by enrollment-driven formulas—a characteristic common to community colleges in all but a few states. Part-time students with skill deficits cost as much or more to serve but bring less in the way of revenues. When this fact is combined with the impact of property tax limitations enacted by the legislature in the state served by the Richfield District, a familiar picture of community college fiscal constraints emerges. Even though the district was relatively affluent as such districts are judged, it still found it necessary to follow the practices that have become so common among community college districts nationwide.

One of these practices was, of course, the heavy and increasing use of low-paid adjunct faculty members. Certainly, this adjustment was apparent at Oakwood, where more than half of all instruction was offered by faculty members in an adjunct status. Although part-time teachers may provide adequate instruction, they do not generally involve themselves in advising or committee work. Where their numbers become an issue with the full-time faculty, as at Oakwood, there may be growing disaffection combined with unwillingness to provide extra advising or other student support formerly taken for granted. The unwillingness of members of the heavily tenured Oakwood faculty to engage in any service or activity for which they were not contracted or did not receive extra compensation had important implications for the implementation of institutional priorities. In these characteristics, Oakwood faculty members were like their counterparts in other community colleges; they differed somewhat in their strong and continuing commitment to their transfer programs, the percentage possessing the doctorate, and the amount of influence they had become accustomed to exercising over the educational program.

Like multicampus districts everywhere, Richfield agonized over the centralization/decentralization dilemma and experienced continuing tensions between campuses and central administration. During the study, the district decentralized a number of support functions and emphasized a commitment to greater campus autonomy. Concurrently, however, an emphasis on standardization within the educational programs and the use of district task forces to plan in specified areas produced greater centralization in the educational program.

On balance, Oakwood and Richfield present a familiar story. Although they have unique characteristics, the overall picture is of a large, comprehensive multicampus community college system vigorously pursuing the priorities and practices associated with districts that aspire to be in the vanguard of community colleges during the 1980s.

CHAPTER THREE

꧁ ꧂ ꧃

Teaching and Learning
in the Classroom

꧁ ꧂ ꧃

By the end of the 1970s, Oakwood College was experiencing the stress that accompanies shifts in the student body and changes in financial and political realities of the external environment. Exacerbating the pressure on faculty members and administrators to cope effectively with these stressors was a highly competent, change-oriented district administration that strongly encouraged Oakwood staff to respond quickly to new students and new environmental forces by changing the educational program.

Adaptation to these demands was manifested in the classroom. In daily face-to-face interactions, students and instructors negotiated what they expected of each other. During this process, classroom literacy demands were implicitly redefined. Because most degrees and certificates required no demonstrated exit competencies beyond the completion of required courses, the literacy standards for the college were ambiguous.

The literacy we observed in most Oakwood classrooms supported our thesis that many current instructional practices in open-access colleges result in a leveling down. This chapter and the next provide a detailed description of classrooms and classroom reading and writing at Oakwood. Then, Chapters Five and Six look more closely at the student and faculty motivations and objectives that shaped the circumstances we observed.

Classroom Research

A growing research tradition looks inside classrooms to analyze interaction between students and teachers and its implications for learning and teaching. This tradition has included prestructured observations carried out by educational psychologists to measure teacher effectiveness in terms of a learning theory that is largely behavioristic (see review by Furlong and Edwards, 1977; Koehler, 1978). These researchers, including especially Amidon (Amidon and Hunter, 1967) and Flanders (1970), have documented the strong influence of the teacher as manipulator and controller of information. Complementing this trend are sociolinguistic and ethnographic studies (see collected works in Gilmore and Smith, 1982; Green and Wallat, 1981; Wilkinson, 1981), which look more broadly and openly at all aspects of classroom activity and use concepts from sociology and anthropology to interpret that activity as social interaction, communication, and cultural transmission. Finally, educational anthropologists have emphasized the need to supplement classroom studies with studies of the classroom's institutional and societal contexts (Ogbu, 1981).

In interpreting our observations of Oakwood classrooms, we have been influenced by these three trends in current work in the field. In particular, we were assisted in our analysis by available frameworks for describing participation structures (Philips, 1972) and event structures (Burnett, 1973; Mehan, 1978; Erickson and Schultz, 1981). In looking at instructors' and students' communication styles, we drew on a sociolinguistic framework (Hymes, 1964), while the work of Mann and his associates (1970) helped to suggest the social roles implied by these styles in college classrooms.

Our results are consistent with similar research in other college classrooms in documenting the influential role of the instructor (Stiles and others, 1979; Cooper, 1981a and 1981b;

Cytrynbaum and Conran, 1979) as well as the mutual negotiation of styles that seems to go on between instructor and students (Dreyfus and Eggleston, 1979; Feldman and Prohaska, 1979; Mann and others, 1970).

At Oakwood there were three types of classrooms, associated with three varieties of classroom literacy. These contrasting classroom environments differed in their physical settings and in the scheduled times within which instructional activities occurred. They were also characterized by differing patterns of social organization and varying styles of learning and teaching.

Most courses at Oakwood could be labeled *information-transfer courses* because their activities had a single focus—the transfer of specific information from instructors to students. The great majority of courses were of this type, regardless of program area or content emphasis. However, two contrasting course types were observed: the *vocational lab course,* directed toward development of job-related skills through involvement in hands-on activities, and the *basic language skills course,* designed to teach basic reading, writing, and speaking skills through structured group activities.

Information-Transfer Courses

Students in information-transfer courses met in square or rectangular classrooms, with writing armchairs arranged in columns. In the front were a blackboard and, usually, a table or lectern. Elementary and secondary classrooms often reflect the personal style of the instructor (Delamont, 1976), but at Oakwood this was usually not so. Because instructors moved from classroom to classroom, there were few personal touches, and because each classroom was used for a variety of courses, there were few subject-related charts or displays. Except for an occasional file cabinet, clock, wall map, or infrequently used bulletin board, classrooms were empty of distractions. The physical setting suggested a single specialized purpose, which we called information transfer.

Information-transfer courses were held regularly in fifty-minute sessions two or three days a week for fifteen weeks.

During each session, content lectures were usually the single predominant activity, although they were often punctuated with brief anecdotal segments and framed by brief introductory and closing remarks.

The regularity and definition of the sessions helped to ensure that instructors succeeded in communicating the knowledge they valued. Concurrently, students were reassured of their ability to meet predictable requirements. The uniformity of such classes reflected their single focus as well as the relative homogeneity of expectations.

The instructors acting as knowledge brokers practiced a teaching style we termed "information dissemination," while modal students served as an attentive audience. This excerpt from one student's account of an economics class provides a good illustration of instructor and student styles in the information-transfer classroom:

> He always starts off his lecture by reviewing what we just discussed the class before. You know, he'll say something like "Well, last time we were talking about the Keynesian theory, and today we'll want to compare this with the classical theory." Sometimes this is a little confusing if you're trying to take notes on what he says, but that doesn't usually really matter so much, because, like me, most students just put into their notes what the instructor writes on the board anyhow. He uses the board a lot to put all his main points on and to go over diagrams, so if you just write down what he puts on the board and maybe add a few remarks he makes in the margins, you have good notes.
>
> Once he starts lecturing, he mostly goes right on through the class period. He knows a lot, a lot more than us, about economics, and he always tries to give us good information on the topic. Usually, a few students will ask him some questions. Mostly they ask him about something on the board or from the text. The instructor answers all questions, but he usually doesn't spend much time. I mean, he's got a lot of material to get us through in just a semester.
>
> So, anyway, that's what usually happens in a

class—the instructor lectures, we listen and take
notes, and some of us answer questions or ask
them. One or two students in the back of the room
I've noticed sleep through most of the class, but
the instructor never says anything.

Instructor Styles. Mann and his associates (1970) described six interpersonal roles portrayed by the teachers they
observed in college lecture classrooms: expert, formal authority,
socializing agent, facilitator, ego ideal, and person. Most often
we observed instructors at Oakwood to embody the expert or
formal authority roles, as indicated by their classroom behaviors.

Instructors carried out predictable activities during content lectures. Typically, they entered the classroom at exactly
the class starting time and went through a series of "rituals" sig-
nifying the beginning of class. These instructors generally had a
"favorite spot," or resting place, where they lectured. From this
location they circumambulated a relatively small area in the
front of the classroom, moving to the lectern, to the blackboard, and back to their resting place. Information disseminators referred to their lecture notes and wrote almost continu-
ously as they spoke, usually on a blackboard but sometimes on
an overhead projector. These physical characteristics of teaching
style emphasized the instructor's central role and aided the
presentation of information.

Oakwood lecturers provided clear transitions between
topics, summarized frequently, and included multiple cues to
important points. They did this by slowing down, increasing
their volume, lowering their pitch, or pausing when key information was presented.

Repetition and paraphrasing were also used liberally.
Consider the paraphrased repetitions in the following excerpt
from a psychology lecture presenting the basic scientific assumption of an orderly universe:

The assumptions of the scientific method
are, first of all, *order,* and by this assumption you
are assuming that the world is *not a haphazard sequence of events* but things *occur in regular sequence.* In other words, things *don't just haphaz-*

ardly happen or *happen at random. There is a pattern* to the phenomenon you're investigating, regardless of what it is. If this weren't true, then there would be no need for science. If things could occur, just always occur, *at random without any pattern* or *in any order,* then there wouldn't ever be a science. We could never discover that *pattern.* Obviously, you have to assume that there is *order* to the universe to have a science. The second assumption . . .

These verbal characteristics were consistent with the instructor's goal of accurately transmitting information to an attentive audience.

A distinctive interaction style was also used to strengthen one-way communication from instructors to students. Instructors gave only general eye contact to the class, sometimes panning the group or focusing on a spot just above or between heads but never actually meeting any individual's glance. Information disseminators did not encourage student questioning during a lecture. They refused to acknowledge would-be questioners until an appropriate transition point, and even then they paused only briefly, often neglecting to look around the room for raised hands. When a question was asked, they gave a brief, concise answer that left little room for further inquiry.

Students seemed to recognize this aspect of instructor style and to accept it because there was so much material to "get through." One student in microbiology commented:

> Sometimes she ignores me. She'll see my hand up and ignore it. Maybe she doesn't have the time—maybe she has something real important to say. . . . You can't have everything. At the university you're never going to ask a question.

Information disseminators seldom reprimanded students who slept, did other work, or talked during the lecture. They usually lectured until the last minute of the class session and ended their lectures abruptly. They did answer student questions after class—but briefly, as they moved toward the door.

Student Styles. Student styles in information-transfer

courses differed in extent of voluntary verbal participation and in degree of engagement in focused classroom activity (Watts, 1981). Most students in the *attentive audience* were "active nonparticipants"—what Mann and others (1970) called the "silent students." Paying just enough attention to recognize points cued by the instructor as important, they sat scattered throughout the classroom, usually not in direct eye contact with the instructor. They responded to the instructor's ritual beginning by opening their notebooks, picking up pens, and ceasing talk. Although they appeared to be listening, they maintained a relaxed posture, gave little obvious nonverbal feedback to the instructor, and never asked questions or voluntarily answered the instructor's questions.

Students in the attentive audience took notes only when the instructor wrote on the board or used the most obvious prosodic cues. Their notes were brief and generally were verbatim reproductions of the instructor's blackboard writings. These students made occasional comments to neighboring students and seemed to be influenced by what other students near them were doing. They often shifted posture and took notes almost simultaneously. At the close of the lecture, they left quickly.

A minority of students constituted a small *responding audience* that engaged in verbal and nonverbal communication with the instructor. The responding audience included both "active participants" and "passive participants." The active participants, sitting in the front of the room, were the most thoroughly engaged in the lecture. They closely monitored the instructor's presentation and took extensive notes. They were responsible for most of the verbal interaction directed to the instructor, although this generally consisted of simple requests for repetition or clarification of content or assignments. The passive participants, often located on the periphery of the classroom, also provided feedback, took extensive notes, and spoke voluntarily, but they were more selective in their participation. Passive participants, though maintaining more distance from the class interaction than their active colleagues, were nonetheless skilled observers, aware of both focused and unfocused activity throughout the classroom.

The responding audience seemed to fulfill a necessary function for the class. Considering the lecture as a dialogue between instructor and class, it was these students who maintained the class side of the exchange. In a sense, the instructor was speaking with them while the rest of the class watched. They became part of the show for the attentive audience. One wonders whether, if there had been no responding audience, the content lecture could have been maintained. If the responding audience had constituted a majority, however, the characteristics of the content lecture would certainly have changed.

Classes usually included a few "passive nonparticipants" who could not be considered part of either the responding or the attentive audience. They did not interact verbally or nonverbally with the instructor, took few notes, and in general paid little attention to the lecture. They might sleep, doodle, or communicate with other students. However, their behavior was tolerated because it did not interfere with the focused activity of the lecture.

Variations in Class Activities. Sometimes the instructor in an information-transfer class deviated from the content lecture. Variations in activity involved anecdotal lectures, audiovisual presentations, and large-group discussions, each of which resulted in changes in instructor and student roles that affected classroom literacy.

When information disseminators moved to more *anecdotal lectures,* they assumed the role of entertainers. They usually moved away from the blackboard and lectern toward the students and looked more directly at the class. The prosodic characteristics of their speech became more dramatic, and humor was introduced. The instructor in a general business course, for example, frequently changed from his clear, emphatic, and rather authoritative content-lecture delivery to a "story mode." His voice dropped quite low and was relatively clipped and quick-paced.

The story mode seemed to serve various functions for instructors. Stories were often told to illustrate the lecture content, to ease anxiety, or to establish better rapport with the class. Because an abrupt change into the story mode could cap-

ture the students' attention, a story might also be told as an indirect response to potentially negative or unwanted classroom
behavior, such as late entry, early departure, or unwanted discussion. Overall, anecdotal lectures seemed to facilitate the in-
formation-dissemination style of instructors. Shifting between
lecture and story modes tended to keep instructors talking and
students listening.

Some anecdotes related more directly to the course content and some less. Degree of relatedness was associated with
variations in the listening behavior of the attentive audience.
During the most related anecdotes, students sat back in their
seats and stopped taking notes, but they still held their pens and
looked intently at the instructor, often offering more nonverbal
feedback than during the content portions of lectures. When
anecdotes were less related, students put down pens, shifted
into very relaxed positions, looked around the room, and even
talked with neighbors.

Information disseminators also used *audiovisual lectures*
occasionally. During such lectures, instructors changed location
and stood in the student portion of the classroom, facing the
front with the students. They did no writing and spoke in a less
highly cued fashion. This lecturing style fell between the anecdotal and content lectures in formality and prosodic characteristics. Students maintained a relaxed position, as they did for an
anecdotal lecture, and usually took no notes. They regarded
audiovisual lectures in a casual manner and in interviews often
spoke of these events as minimally useful to their classroom experiences. In microbiology, for example, most students did not
take notes when the instructor used overhead transparencies.
They looked at the screen and their own handouts but did not
write on their copies. One student explained, "If it's too hard
for her to draw on the board, we won't have it on a test."

An audiovisual lecture in an American history course presented an extreme case of student inattention:

> He puts a transparency on the overhead at
> about 10:30. Clare gets up to turn off the light.
> The instructor is barely audible now in the back of

the room. His voice has to compete with the fan motor on the projector, the air conditioner, and a movie in the next room. One row up and two rows over, Jean and Mary seize the opportunity and begin an animated conversation. The instructor puts on another transparency at 10:40. Five heads are down on desks, presumably asleep. At 10:42, the first of five students to eventually leave the lecture walks out. Clare pokes me in the arm and points to sleepy Don, two people up from me. His head is bobbing dangerously backward and forward. At one point, he comes so far back that his head almost falls on Theresa's books. Clare, John, Betty, Theresa, and I are all watching him intently to see which way he'll fall. Even Michelle comes out of her novel to watch. Finally, his head plops down on his own desk with a small thud—out for the count. We all chuckle. Michelle returns to her novel, and the rest return to their work sheets. The room is still dark at 10:50, and the instructor is on his third or fourth transparency.

When instructors presented audiovisuals without lecturing, student participative styles were similar. As the general content was repetitive of lectures already given, the audiovisuals seemed to serve a supplementary or illustrative purpose. Instructors showed films, videotapes, or slides simply as a way of varying the class sessions. Use of audiovisual forms of presentation may have served a secondary social function by softening the information-giver/receiver relationship of teacher and student. The instructor often sat with students during the presentation and afterward could talk with them as a fellow information receiver, sharing reactions and interpretations.

The *large-group discussions* that occurred in the information-transfer classroom were "discussions" only in outward form. Although participants called these events discussions, students' contributions were minimal and highly structured. The instructor controlled the flow of the exchange, which usually resembled the triangular pattern that Mehan (1978) and his associates have described as typical of elementary instruction. One student seldom communicated directly with another; rather, most communications flowed exclusively through the instructor. Very few students participated, a fact that further qualifies the use of the term *group discussions* to describe these events. Most students treated this event much like an audiovisual presentation. They sat back, casually following the flow of activity but taking no notes. Only a few active participants spoke, making themselves part of the performance passively observed by their classmates.

The information-transfer course was oriented toward efficient communication of specific facts from instructor to students. Teaching and learning styles reflected this one-way transfer of low-level knowledge, and all aspects of the classroom context facilitated this goal.

Vocational Lab Courses

As previously noted, not all classrooms at Oakwood fit the foregoing description. A minority of courses were more task-oriented and involved more active student participation. Including technical and clerical courses as well as selected courses in the arts and sciences, these were labeled "vocational lab courses" because they were job-specific and focused on "laboratory"-type applied projects. Not all courses designated as vocational in the catalogue were of this type; many were oriented toward information transfer. Similarly, some courses involving laboratory activities did not fit this category, because they used hands-on experiences more for illustrative purposes than to develop vocational skills.

The relatively few courses at Oakwood that were both vocational and lab-oriented had their own characteristic settings and unique styles of teaching and learning. These classrooms were activity- or equipment-oriented. In some instances, the shape and size of the room correlated with the nature of the tasks. Equipment and furniture were distinctive. An automotives class, for example, took place in a high-ceilinged garage where activities centered on a changing assortment of cars and trucks.

Vocational lab classes met for long class periods of several hours. Each lab session was a complex event with many sub-events embedded within it. These events varied for each student. In addition, activities varied greatly from day to day. Beginnings and endings were often vague and drawn out. Because activities were individual and task-dependent, students did not start and stop together. The students arranged themselves in loosely structured work groups in order to facilitate role assignments, communication, and sharing of written materials and equipment.

As students worked on assigned tasks, they interacted in small groups, independent of the instructor. When the instructor did interact with a group, it was usually at students' request. Only during test situations did the instructor initiate a more drill-like arrangement by requiring each student in a group to demonstrate proficiency at a task.

In vocational lab courses, the instructor's style was that of a "guide" or a "resource" for students, who became "workers." As the instructor in an office machines course said, "Remember, girls, this is a job. Your pay is the skill you take home." Circulating throughout the classroom, the instructor responded to students' needs, answered questions, demonstrated, explained, questioned students, or evaluated their performance. Rather than following a preset agenda, activities were often spontaneous, responding to the specific needs of students. In interactions with students, instructors emphasized not only skills and knowledge related to the activity at hand but also attitudes and more general sociocultural competencies associated with the work environment being simulated in the classroom.

The following description of the office machines class illustrates the teaching and learning styles in a vocational lab course:

> When I arrived, most of the students were already seated at their machines and had started working. . . . Ms. Krono was demonstrating to students working on the editing typewriter. She said, "If you've read the book, and I hope you did, you'll recognize this." Before she started demonstrating to the editing typewriter section, she col-

lected materials for the duplicating section and got them started. As Ms. Krono was explaining to the editing typewriter group, Lois noticed something on her Executive typewriter and called all the other women around her, plus Fay. . . . Meanwhile, Laura had jumped up to help Lucy three times. She tried verbally to explain, first, but this didn't work; she had to get up and explain it to her. . . .

In the transcription area, Sue Ellen told Veronica, "No, it's *i* before *e* except after *c*." All three of them compared their letters for style. Sue Ellen said, "I know. Doesn't it look like it should be down a little farther?" The folder that accompanied the tape that they type from explains whom the letter was from, the letter style, suggested margins, the date on which it was to be typed, and so on.

Three of the duplicating girls looked for materials. They were illustrating and typing poems to duplicate on ditto. At 8:25, the instructor became aware that the transcription girls were having problems. Sue Ellen's tape was erased halfway through. Ms. Krono said, "Okay, girls, what's your problem?" She investigated.

Meanwhile, Faye and Ruth were quizzing each other on the parts of the ditto machine with a diagram, since the ditto was broken. . . .

Instructor Styles. Instructors in vocational lab courses had a very direct, straightforward style of complete accessibility to students at all times. Their primary role was to demonstrate, explain, and help students solve problems for themselves. In one automotives course, for example, the instructor assumed an advising role. He was there to answer questions and to provide assistance with special problems students might have. If there were no questions, he would not demand anything until it was time to check students' work for credit. Most of his advice was in the form of a demonstration or in working with a student to solve a problem. In one microbiology course, the instructor's style in lab differed from her style in lecture. One student commented, "In the lab, she's interested and answers questions. . . . She's a little more laid-back and more easy. I guess that's because she's working more with students."

Student Styles. Students in their role as "workers" were expected to take on much responsibility. Assignments were vague but implied, evaluations passive but watchful. Instructors emphasized "independence" in student behavior. As one student in an advanced psychology lab commented, "I realized that the teacher, although an extremely nice, fun guy, was determined to make the students do everything themselves."

In occupational lab courses, students often seemed to be more intrinsically motivated. For example, in the automotives course, everybody enjoyed working on cars; students showed pride in workmanship and strove for thorough knowledge of what they were working on. They enjoyed the ample time provided to work on cars as well as the facilities where they worked. They had great respect for the instructor's knowledge and enjoyed his attitude and his treatment of them. The students seemed to gain strength from being in a program where they could escape to the solitude of the garage and where they were treated fairly and were allowed to share knowledge freely.

In some labs of information-transfer courses, however, students' orientation toward the course made the worker role less acceptable. In microbiology, most students were taking the course because it was required in a nursing program. The labs did not deal with skills related to their goals. Very few students, if any, had an interest in laboratory research. Consequently, the lab took on a different function: It served to illustrate the information presented in lecture. Although students did "work" in groups on lab activities, using the instructor as a resource, their performance was not critical. Evaluation came from lab quizzes, which relied on the instructor as information disseminator. In experimental psychology, which was also oriented toward information transfer, students balked at the instructor's insistence on student independence. They seemed to find this expectation unfair:

> The instructor hasn't explained assignments thoroughly. . . . I don't feel he taught us well. I really had to teach myself.

In the true vocational labs, student-to-student interaction

became highly important and was perhaps the most critical student strategy for learning. Several types of interaction among students were observed in work-group sessions. The first type was "showing how." Students serving as resources would demonstrate a procedure or check out someone else's equipment to find the source of a problem. In "telling how," the resource person might explain a procedure rather than do it or might offer an interpretation of written or oral instructions. Students also "monitored" other students' work. They watched while someone tried to perform a task and caught the other student when he or she made a mistake. Sometimes they monitored verbally by asking a series of questions such as "Did you check the plug?" "Did you adjust the bottom dial?" More complex patterns of interaction were also observed, such as "explaining while demonstrating" or "explaining while watching" someone else perform a task. Finally, in "mutual monitoring," two students might go through a procedure simultaneously until their actions diverged. Then they would try to resolve their differences.

Variations in Class Activities. Laboratory sessions sometimes included demonstration drills and demonstration lectures. During a *demonstration lecture* the instructor took on the style of a "model" of appropriate skilled behavior. The students became "vicarious participants" who watched intently but generally did not ask questions or take notes. During *demonstration drills* students were required to manipulate concrete objects or equipment for the instructor. Such a demonstration drill was the basic form of evaluation.

> As far as evaluation is concerned, Mr. Knight has a checklist with everyone's name on it and columns running across the top indicating the work done. Everyone is responsible for one single-barrel, two two-barrels, two four-barrels, an idle adjustment by ear, and an idle adjustment with the infrared. This is a hell of a lot of work, and this includes finding the carburetor to use, whether it means taking it off your own car during class or doing other people's. A carburetor is considered done

when the things I have already mentioned have been done, plus all of the external adjustments. These adjustments are described in various service manuals and on the specifications sheet included with the carburetor kit. Mr. Knight considers these adjustments of prime importance and is carefully monitoring each guy's work.

The vocational lab course, then, focused on the accomplishment of defined tasks within a simulated work environment. Teaching and learning in this type of class were assisted by the environment as well as by the ongoing informal interaction among students and between instructor and students.

Basic Language Skills Courses

In contrast to courses oriented toward information transfer or task performance, a small number of courses were designed to develop basic language skills. Because these courses enrolled a preponderance of nontraditional students, they emphasized the development of classroom behavior and attitudes considered appropriate for college students.

The physical setting for basic language skills courses was student-oriented. Although the classrooms were similar in size and shape to the rooms used for information-transfer courses, the furniture was flexibly and irregularly arranged. Students, sitting at desks or tables, clustered together according to such attributes as ethnicity, age, sex, and interest. These clusters became multiple foci for classroom activity. The front of the room, a center of attention in information-transfer courses, was often ignored in basic language skills courses as instructors moved about in the students' space.

Basic language (and some math) skills courses met as often as four or five times a week and occasionally for sessions as long as those in the vocational lab courses. Some basic skills courses began with an activity involving the whole group, such as an anecdotal lecture or a drill, but most commonly several events occurred simultaneously, and transitions between activities were not clearly marked. The instructor might conduct a text-dependent drill with one group while other students worked individually or in small groups with tutor assistance.

When instructors initiated interactions with student groups, they required each student to respond individually while the rest of the class listened. This arrangement, which has often been found in elementary schools, occurred at Oakwood only in the basic skills courses, where it dominated class events whether these were labeled recitations, drills, or discussions.

The dependence of students on their instructors was underscored both by the drill activity and by the variability of the simultaneous events occurring in the classroom. In contrast to information-transfer courses, where patterns were predictable, students in the basic language skills classes neither controlled their own participation nor were able to predict what would happen next. The following excerpt, describing an intensive English as a Second Language course, illustrates the group learning and teaching activity of the basic language skills courses.

> I arrived at the classroom at about 1:00 P.M. The students were working in three groups, and at times the noise level got very loud. This was especially true when several groups were working on oral exercises. One section of seven students was writing sentences from the cards. The cards were pictures of different things that are found around the home. On one side of the card, which was about 8½ X 11, was the picture, and on the other side was the same picture, but the name of the thing was also printed—for example, *cabinet*. The aide held up the card, then asked the student what the thing was. The student was then asked to say what the thing was used for. These cards consisted of items such as television, stairs, telephone, teapot, desk, or lamp.
>
> Another section was working from their workbooks. These six students were writing the exercises that deal with where people get services, such as the bank, general store, post office. In these exercises, the students copied an example from the workbook, and then they filled in the sentences like the examples. During these exercises, the

aide circulated among the students and corrected them as the student finished the exercises.

The third section was working on verbal communication. They were practicing speaking the "I ams." The conversation would involve a student doing something and saying what he was doing. Don got up and walked around his desk. He then stated, "I am walking around the desk." The students in the group then responded, "You are walking around the desk." Some of the other examples used were "I am talking"; "I am sitting at the desk."

The three groups continued working on the above exercises until 1:45 P.M. They were then given a break. At 2:00, a counselor came, and he was going to work with the students who needed to fill out their financial aid packets.

In basic language skills courses, all students were obliged to participate and were constantly supervised. Instructors were interested in socializing students by getting them to perform appropriately in the classroom. To accomplish their objectives, instructors in language skills courses took on the style of directors (or, as Mann and others, 1970, might say, "socializers"), while students became obligatory respondents.

Instructor Styles. During guided workbook activities, for example, the instructor would briefly introduce the skill to be practiced and then call on various students to read introductory materials, examples, and problems from the class workbook. After a student had spoken, the instructor would repeat and evaluate the answer, sometimes writing the correct response on the blackboard. Although instructors sometimes called for voluntary responses at the beginning of class activities, eventually they began to call on all members of the group. Instructors might stand at the front of the group but would be careful to have eye contact with each member, perhaps walking among the students, sitting close, or directing a specific glance. Instructors were often aware of the verbal and nonverbal behavior of each group member and watched to see whether individuals wrote in their workbooks at appropriate times.

Student Styles. During drills, students, as obligatory participants, followed in their workbooks as the instructor and other students spoke. When answers were given and were evaluated by the instructor, the students would transcribe or copy these into their own workbooks. Students had to follow the verbal interchange carefully not only to be able to write correct answers but also to be able to respond appropriately when their turn came.

Variations in Class Activities. Even activities during which students completed worksheets and workbook pages included social elements and reflected the same teaching and learning styles as drill activities. Students sat in groups and talked with other students and with tutors who initiated and structured much of the interaction.

Small-group discussions also illustrated the instructors' objective of socializing students and their greater emphasis on affective objectives. Instructors regularly engaged students in group discussions, telling them the activity would help them become more "considerate," "tolerant," and "responsible"—all aspects of appropriate classroom attitude and behavior. On one occasion, when the students did not stay on topic and could not express clear opinions, the instructor gave the class a lecture on "civic responsibility." Students in basic language skills were aware of the affective objectives behind discussion activities. Some seemed to accept this purpose as legitimate and became active participants, while others did not value the group discussions and participated only as required.

The basic language skills courses, though ostensibly oriented toward developing reading and writing skills, showed a strong focus on socialization. Both teaching and learning styles seemed to indicate agreement with this implicit purpose for the course experience. The physical and temporal setting reflected a highly structured student-centered but instructor-directed environment.

Summary Discussion

We have described the typical Oakwood classroom as devoted to information transfer. This designation might apply to most college classrooms across the country. In fact, postsecondary education has been said to have "institutionalized but a single mode of learning. Many teachers impart abstract knowledge, divorced from feeling and action through classroom lectures and discussion. Learners assume relatively passive roles" (Fund for the Improvement of Postsecondary Education, 1973, p. 6). A recent study of teaching in forty-two university and community college classrooms showed the instructors lecturing 65 percent of the time and students talking only 35 percent (Johnson and McNamara, 1980). A study by the Center for the Study of Community Colleges (1978b) found that 94–96 percent of instructors in the humanities and sciences lecture for an average of 46 percent of class time. Although community colleges have advocated the use of varying media, these were seldom used, being regarded as supplementary. Class discussions were used by the majority of instructors and accounted for about 20 percent of class time. However, without qualitative data on such discussions, we do not know to what extent they represented genuine dialogue, rather than the perfunctory exchanges observed at Oakwood.

The existence of a few basic skills classes and vocational classes at Oakwood is also not a new revelation. Such classrooms have been described in community college literature before and their unique character recognized. In addition, the fact that evidence of critical literacy was absent from most, if not all, classrooms is not surprising to those familiar with such settings. The Oakwood study, however, like the case studies of open-access colleges presented by London (1978), Roueche and Comstock (1981), and Shor (1980), helps to illuminate the dynamics of these classrooms and explain the role that written language took on within them.

The three types of courses described in this chapter were shaped by an ongoing process of negotiation between instructors and students within an institution emphasizing open access and expanding enrollments. In the dominant type of course, this negotiation process produced a narrow focus on the efficient transfer of low-level, specific information. The negotiation process had taken a different direction in two other contrasting course types, each of which comprised only a small percentage of courses. Vocational lab courses emphasized simulated work experience; students learned rather specific job-related competencies "by doing," and peer interaction and independence from instructor direction were stressed. In basic language skills courses, in contrast, nontraditional students were socialized in a classroom environment that in many ways resembled an elementary school setting. Instructors directed all activities, and students were required to participate in social interaction.

These three environments reflected the institution's attempt to accommodate a new clientele less oriented toward a traditional college education and a faculty that, either by choice or by default, identified less and less with the traditional role of college instructor. Most students were seen by themselves and others as passive recipients of knowledge, apprentice workers, or dependent respondents in the classroom, while most faculty members were viewed as information disseminators, resource persons, or directors.

Within each of these classroom environments, norms of literate activity were established. Students came to use written language in ways consistent with their own goals and appropriate for a classroom context. In the next chapter we turn to a consideration of the goal-directed, context-dependent forms of reading and writing that predominated in Oakwood classrooms.

CHAPTER FOUR

❧ ❧ ❧

Reading and Writing Requirements

❧ ❧ ❧

Extensive use of written language may be uncommon in most community college classrooms. A recent study of instructional practices (Cohen and Brawer, 1981) reported that while nearly all instructors used textbooks, they assigned an average of three to four hundred pages a semester (less than thirty pages a week). Fewer than a third required additional readings in outside reference materials, although a majority did provide a brief syllabus and some handout materials in class. Quick-score objective exams were the most common mode of student evaluation, along with in-class essay exams. Fewer than one third of the instructors required term papers or reports of any kind.

Secondary school classrooms have apparently also dropped or changed the requirements for reading and writing. The National Assessment of Educational Progress (1981) has found that students are seldom asked to interpret or summarize extended prose, that most tests ask only for literal recall. Not surprisingly, students' skills at the level of interpretation and synthesis are decreasing. In a study of recent high school graduates in Florida (McCabe and Skidmore, 1982), fewer than half the students reported using a library more than five times in high school or taking more than five essay tests. Fewer than one in six reported being required to read more than fifty pages a week. These students did not expect greater demands as they entered postsecondary education.

Our observations in Oakwood classrooms indicate a similar restriction in reading and writing. This chapter describes Oakwood students' use of written language and points out the characteristics that distinguish it from the type of reading and writing we advocate as necessary for the development of critical literacy.

Collecting data on classroom reading and writing was not an easy task. Because so much of the reading and writing was embedded integrally into ongoing activities, it was often overlooked by students and instructors alike. For example, when asked whether any in-class writing occurred, many students said no until directly questioned about taking notes. Then they would agree that they did in fact write in class. Similarly, at first students said they never read the textbook but then, on probing, described how they used the text in studying for tests. For our purposes, we explain this almost unconscious use of reading and writing by considering these uses of written language "operations," which occur in the service of goal-directed activity and are not themselves the subject of much attention (Leont'ev, 1974).

The operations we observed in Oakwood classrooms can be described along a number of simple dimensions borrowed and freely adapted from available sociolinguistic frameworks (Hymes, 1964). *Channel* refers to a medium of communication and is used to distinguish among operations involving written language (reading and writing), oral language (listening and speaking), and nonverbal communication (observing and manipulating). Operations can also be distinguished by whether they involve producing or receiving information. By cross-classifying these two dimensions, we catalogued as follows the communications we observed in Oakwood classrooms:

- *Productive written*—writing
- *Productive oral*—speaking

- *Productive nonverbal*—manipulating
- *Receptive written*—reading
- *Receptive oral*—listening
- *Receptive nonverbal*—observing

We used these categories to identify the classroom activities that involved the use of written language as an operation. Once identified, written language use could be further categorized using two other dimensions: the form in which language was presented, from discrete to continuous; and the degree of explicitness of the cues provided to meaning, from very specific to very general. Using these dimensions, two maximally contrasting categories of written language use could be described.

The first of these we termed *texting*. Texting involves the use of reading and writing to comprehend or compose connected language without the assistance of specific cues. Examples are reading a textbook chapter to gain an overview of the important events of the 1920s and writing an essay that argues for or against capital punishment. Texting represents a traditional (liberal arts) view of the type of written language use that colleges should promote and should expect their students to demonstrate. Consistent with this traditional view, the students we interviewed described themselves as "really reading" and "really writing" only when they were dealing independently with connected language.

In contrast to texting were operations we designated as *bitting*. Bitting was the use of reading or writing to understand or produce fragmented language when presented with specific external cues. Students were bitting when they read and copied from the blackboard a list of names that the instructor pointed to and identified as important and when they later recognized these names on a multiple-choice test. They were engaged in a somewhat more independent form of bitting when they skimmed a textbook to find answers to study-guide questions in preparation for a multiple-choice test. Bitting might involve either connected discourse (a textbook) or disconnected discourse (a list of names or definitions). In both instances, however, an information source was used to obtain fragments of meaning, and strong external cues were present.

The reading and writing observed at Oakwood approximated bitting closely enough to justify the generalization that bitting had become the norm for classroom written language. This was true in each of the three course types identified in Chapter Three, although there were unique characteristics of literacy in each setting.

Reading and Writing in Three Types of Classrooms

Information-Transfer Courses. In information-transfer courses, notegiving and notetaking were the characteristic reading/writing behaviors that facilitated one-way communication from instructor to students. Written language was a tool to help this interaction run more smoothly. Instructors used written language in class to make their presentation accessible to the whole group and to support their position as the single focus of attention. Students' use of written language in notetaking kept them in the role of receptive audience.

Students reported a number of reasons for notetaking. Some were making a record for use in studying for a test or as a guide to help in reading the text. Some were just using the notetaking activity to help themselves pay attention and to prevent boredom. Some simply said they took notes because the students around them did, and others admitted they had never thought about their reasons; notetaking was just what one did during a lecture.

Even the nature and arrangement of furniture and equipment facilitated the use of reading and writing in the dissemination of information. The instructor was encouraged to read from notes and write out key terms and concepts by the easy availability of a lectern and blackboard space. The writing armchairs facing the blackboard in evenly spaced columns emphasized the undifferentiated nature of the group and announced the student's role as notetaker.

Writing was not a factor, however, whenever storytelling, audiovisuals, or discussions became the focus of classroom activity. Perhaps the reason was that reading and writing were not considered appropriate for these supplementary activities or that these forms of interaction were thought of as peripheral to the main goal of the course, information transfer.

Outside class, students used written language only to prepare for in-class examinations, most of which were multiple-choice tests requiring literal recognition and recall of specific information. Though working independently, the students relied heavily on cues to importance given by instructors during lectures, as well as in written study guides. Students typically read their textbooks once through in a casual fashion to get an overall feel for the chapters or just to "get through" them. Then, when they studied for tests, they used notes, handouts, and textbooks in a skimming fashion in order to prepare to recognize specific information on multiple-choice tests. They could expect that few, if any, test items would require them to analyze, synthesize, or evaluate the information.

An analysis of the written materials used in information-transfer classes at Oakwood revealed the extent to which these materials were oriented toward bitting. In fact, many of them would have been difficult to "text." However, even in classes in which materials did seem suitable for texting, students read them in a texting manner only during the early part of a semester. As the semester progressed, interviews suggested a decreasing incidence of independent texting even by the most active participants in a course. Students soon discovered that tests could be passed with minimal reading. Thereafter, they did only the necessary bitting.

A small number of students did use reading and writing more elaborately in a "texting" fashion. When they took notes, they often tried to restructure and rewrite board notes in their own way. Because these few students read the relevant sections of the textbook before a lecture, they usually constituted the small responding audience in the classroom, prepared to answer and ask questions. The students in this responding audience used reading and writing to aid the acquisition of knowledge that they found interesting and valuable. Many of them enjoyed the process of learning itself and so gained satisfaction from carrying out reading and writing activities that they associated with a student role. However, because these students were in the minority, the literacy norms negotiated in Oakwood classrooms reflected not their style but the far more restricted "bitting" style of the majority in the attentive audience.

Basic Language Skills Courses. In basic language skills courses, reading and writing occurred within the social context of guided interaction. Instructors as socializers in a directive role did not want students to waste time on activities geared to information transfer, nor did they wish to require students to engage in much reading and writing outside a social context. The students, for their part, also preferred to do their writing and reading in the classroom under the instructor's direction, because they were unfamiliar with the content, form, and function of the reading and writing tasks in which they were engaged.

Typically, all course work was completed during class time. Reading and writing were used in completing workbook exercises and in drills conducted within a group setting under instructor or tutor guidance. Students were seldom asked to deal with more than a phrase or a brief sentence at a time, and their use of written language was constantly monitored. The student-centered arrangement of the classroom and the variable use of time facilitated this directed, social variety of literacy.

Vocational Lab Courses. In vocational lab courses, reading and writing were used whenever they contributed to the work being done. Students referred to manuals and written instructions as they tried to carry out tasks. Often, students shared their interpretations of the instructions and discussed the application to the current problem. The written word was a tool but seldom the final authority.

Vocational labs seem to operate largely according to an oral tradition—but an oral tradition supplemented by the selected use of written language. One researcher's description of the automotives class he observed illustrated this point:

> We followed the service manual and were able to do most of the adjustments. However,

when troubles occurred, we fell back on more in-
tuitive modes of work. Final adjustments were
made by ear and feel rather than by what we had
read in the manual. Taking this kind of written advice is all well and good, but the final verification
or trust is ultimately put in how things sound or
look. There is a whole set of criteria that will finally satisfy a good mechanic, but these things are not
easily presented in written form.

To do well, a student in such a tradition has to be able to
read, listen, observe, and share experiences with other students
and the teacher. After a time, it becomes evident to learners
that they will hear, see, or read important aspects of required
knowledge a great number of times. With patience they will obtain the information as long as they are paying attention, without need for much use of written language.

"Bitting" in the Classroom

Although reading and writing were common activities in
Oakwood classrooms, the use of written language was restricted
in the way it was carried out and in the functions it seemed to
serve. This minimal use may be typical of the extent to which
written language use in open-access colleges is coming to resemble uses found among the general public, in contrast to the uses
traditionally associated with higher learning.

First, the reading and writing that occurred were not of a
type that could be used to communicate information by itself.
Instead, reading and writing were used along with oral language
and contextual cues and occurred as part of social interaction.
This multimodal characteristic of literacy has been described as
a primary aspect of modern society. Ong (1980) described the
"secondarily oral tradition" we live with today. In a secondarily
oral tradition, no single channel of communication is emphasized; people seek to transfer information by repetition and
multiple modes. Dubois (1980) asserts that the greatest challenge for linguists today is to understand this current norm, the
joint use of written and oral language.

Nor is the social-contextual integration of written language that we observed unusual. Heath (1982) found, in her study of literacy in home settings, that although the community was considered literate, most of the reading and writing occurred during social interactions. Reading and writing almost never stood alone. Individuals did virtually no solitary reading except when elderly men and women read their Bible alone. Heath also reported that families' literacy habits did not match those usually attributed to fully literate groups. Parents did not read to their children, encourage conversation about books, or write or read extended prose passages. Reading was not an individual pursuit, nor was it considered to have intellectual, esthetic, or critical rewards.

A third characteristic of the written language we observed was its disconnected form. Most of the writing produced by students and much of what they read was presented in discrete words and phrases. However, this characteristic in itself may not be alarming. Scribner and Jacob (1980), Mikulecky and Diehl (1979), and Jacob and Crandall (1979) all report the abbreviated nature of most writing used in job settings. As in the Oakwood research, these researchers found that people often failed to report much of the reading and writing they did because it had become so integrated into everyday tasks and also because its form did not fit their conception of "real" reading and writing:

> Literacy activities may involve reading and writing short-term notes and messages, filing and retrieving information from documents to answer a short question over the telephone. These would rarely be identified as literacy activities by people performing them, yet they require reading and writing, and, in fact, they occur frequently during the workday. It is these kinds of activities which people often discount as "not really reading" [Jacob and Crandall, p. 3, n. 3].

Of course, we were observing in an academic setting, not in the job environment, where the uses reported by these authors seem much more appropriate.

Bits of written language can be used as part of thoughtful, autonomous activity. Individuals often do use pieces of language as input as they go about creative problem solving, critical evaluation, and a search for holistic meanings. This realization, however, brings us closer to the source of our discontent with the reading and writing we observed at Oakwood and with much of what is reported in other educational settings.

The information communicated through written language remained as bits of isolated fact. It was not integrated or analyzed to achieve more holistic meaning. The college students we observed did not read textbooks to grasp both major themes and supportive detail, nor did they listen actively and critically to lectures and record comprehensive notes. Oakwood students were not required to synthesize, analyze, or evaluate information from texts and lectures. Instead, they learned discrete pieces of information in order to recognize or reproduce them intact on objective exams.

In addition, student reading and writing were highly dependent activities, shaped by the general nature of students' roles in the classroom. The most typical form of social interaction involved students serving as attentive audience, and in this situation students used reading and writing as part of passive, receptive activity. Concurrently, in the basic language skills courses, reading and writing became little more than procedures that students performed under the direction of watchful instructors. Only in the less numerous vocational lab courses did the use of written language acquire any degree of independence, although it was quite minimal and was integrated into the "job" activities of the "worker" students.

In many classrooms, written language was in danger of becoming merely procedural, losing its true communicative function. Bloome (1981) described this danger in a study of one student's reading behavior in a junior high school classroom, noting that the student had been learning "patterns of surface-level behavior that allowed her to participate in some written language events without necessarily having to use written language to effectively communicate over space and time . . . she has learned them procedurally and not substantively" (p. 18).

Summary Discussion

Community college classrooms like those at Oakwood
might be praised for their movement toward a more modern,
relevant use of written language as part of multimodal, context-
ually appropriate and socially integrated activity, as well as for
their adoption of efficient and abbreviated forms of written
communication. This praise must be qualified, however, when
we recognize the lack of critical thinking required of students
and the dependent role they assumed as learners.

Texting forms of reading and writing are valuable precisely because they require analysis, synthesis, and evaluation,
as well as providing the opportunity for students to express
original opinions. It has been through written language that students performed much of their active learning. Now these forms
of written language are being dropped, and no new forms of
analytic and independent communication and information processing are being substituted. The result is a "silencing" of student expression and a lack of opportunity for students to engage in critical thinking. What is alarming is not simply the
change in the form of written language or a diminution of the
amount of reading and writing. Rather, it is the use of written
language, and all language, in a noncritical and dependent manner.

To discover why written language operations were being
used in this restricted way, we need to expand our discussion
from a focus on operations to a focus on literacy. According to
the transactional definition presented in Chapter One, literacy
involves the goal-directed use of written language. Not only do
people use written language in ways appropriate to their roles
in varying contexts, but they do so for identifiable purposes. In
fact, in a transactional view of literacy, goals and objectives are
key factors in explaining changes in the functions that written
language played for students and instructors. For this reason,
Chapters Five and Six turn to a discussion of the course objectives of instructors and the motives of students.

CHAPTER FIVE

ᕤᕮ᠑ ᕤᕮ᠑ ᕤᕮ᠑

Effects of Instructor Objectives on Literacy

ᕤᕮ᠑ ᕤᕮ᠑ ᕤᕮ᠑

Although the norms for classroom activities, as described in Chapters Three and Four, were jointly determined by instructors and students, instructors were expected to set instructional objectives, determine instructional methods, and evaluate learning. There was a strong relation between how instructors performed these activities and the learning strategies that students adopted. Student learning strategies, in turn, determined the students' conception of classroom literacy as well as their opportunities to develop literacy skills. Sticht (1978), in analyzing job literacy in military settings, suggested that students in courses emphasizing psychomotor objectives engage in different literacy behaviors (reading to learn to do) than students in courses emphasizing low-level cognitive objectives (reading to learn the facts). Our study confirmed that course objectives and students' use of reading and writing covary. Therefore, a consideration of instructors' objectives is critical to understanding why bitting was the norm in Oakwood classrooms.

Course objectives refer to student behaviors that represent the intended outcomes of the educational process—that is, "the ways in which individuals . . . act, think, or feel as the result of participating in some unit of instruction" (Bloom, 1956, p. 12). We used a modified form of task analysis to determine the instructors' objectives for the courses observed by our research team.

Our analysis was based on Bloom's three-part taxonomy of educational objectives. The classification scheme consists of cognitive, affective, and psychomotor domains. The *cognitive* domain comprises six levels pertaining to "the recall or recognition of knowledge and the development of intellectual abilities and skills." The *affective* domain comprises five levels related to "changes in interest, attitudes, and values and the development of appreciations and adequate adjustment." The *psychomotor* domain comprises six levels concerned with manipulative skills, motor skills, and acts requiring neuromuscular coordination, ranging from reflex movements to skilled movements and non-discussive communication (Krathwohl, Bloom, and Masia, 1964; Harrow, 1972). Following classification of each objective into one of the three domains, objectives were further classified by level. Levels are arranged in an ascending order of difficulty, with one representing the lowest, or easiest, level.

Course Objectives and Instructor Style

Instructors' teaching styles were related to their emphasis on the various types of objectives. Instructors who concentrated on cognitive objectives generally took on the style of information disseminators. Those who emphasized affective objectives were more likely to resemble the directors we observed in basic language classes. Psychomotor objectives were associated with the guide/resource style of instructors in vocational lab courses.

The course objectives of an information disseminator were illustrated by the comments of a history instructor:

> [I hope that] . . . the students gain a basic understanding of history and that they will have the basic information. . . . My primary method of instruction is lecture. I give handouts on outstanding topics, things that are particularly important.

The course objectives of a guide were reflected in the comments of a business statistics teacher:

> [I stress] . . . application of all problems in class using calculating equipment in real-world context and interpretation of the results from a vast array of problems, from a variety of business fields. . . . I begin with an overview and then I structure the problem. Then we do specific problems on the board. Then I assign them similar problems to do independently on their own. I use the lecture/demonstration method to designate orally what is important for them to know how to do.

The course objectives of a socializer were exemplified by a basic skills instructor:

> She felt that students needed special training to ready them for college. "They must be taught to notice." She further felt a strong obligation to provide social instruction to the students "to build character." Movies were shown to build character and teach tolerance.

Although there was considerable variability, classes observed at Oakwood emphasized cognitive objectives. This is not surprising, as the modal course type at Oakwood was an information-transfer course. Over all courses, more than 40 percent of *all* objectives fell into the first level of the cognitive domain (knowledge), about 30 percent fell into the second and third levels (comprehension and application), and fewer than 5 percent were related to the highest levels of the cognitive domain (analysis, synthesis, and evaluation).

Knowledge objectives involved giving "evidence that one remembered, either by recalling or recognizing, some idea or phenomenon with which [one] has had experience in the educational process" (Bloom, 1956, p. 28). In other words, knowledge was little more than rote recall or recognition of an idea or phenomenon. This emphasis on rote remembering as an end in itself differentiates knowledge from higher levels in the cognitive domain. At these higher levels, knowledge is of little value unless one can use it in new situations or in a different form. Examples of course objectives at the knowledge level included these:

- Recognize the following: Huguenots, Iroquois, New France, Jesuit missionary, King William's War, Queen Anne's War.
- Know the number of grams of fat in a fat exchange.
- Recognize basic statistical notations used in the text.
- Know the order of basic mathematical operations.
- Recognize that raw frontier conditions caused distinctly American traits to develop, particularly as regards democracy.
- Recognize the most important desirable properties of money.

Knowledge-level cognitive objectives thus involved the recall of "isolable bits of information" and, hence, were consistent with our definition of the bitting form of reading and writing. The extensive reliance on this level and category of objective represented a trend at Oakwood supporting the concerns we have expressed about the lack of critical literacy.

Why So Many Knowledge Objectives?

One factor promoting the use of knowledge-level cognitive objectives was the continuing view of a majority of Oakwood instructors that the primary mission of the school was to educate students for transfer to a four-year college or university. As a feeder institution, Oakwood had an obligation to teach the basic knowledge of the disciplines if its transfers were to compete successfully with students who had completed their first two years in a university. Concern for the success of transfer students resulted in efforts to shape the content of transfer courses according to the corresponding programs at the local state university. Perhaps this emphasis on transferable content rather than transferable skills has been a mistake.

A second, related factor is that many Oakwood faculty

members maintained strong disciplinary biases. Others have noted the disciplinary, as opposed to teaching, orientation of community college faculty members. Most faculty members in community colleges have a master's degree in the subject area they teach, but few, if any, have course work dealing with their particular level of teaching, even when such programs have been available (Cohen and Brawer, 1982). When provisions for in-service training have been discussed, faculty members have preferred courses in their subject area offered at universities rather than workshops on instruction or institutional issues (O'Banion, 1971). Instructors saw their responsibilities as acquainting students with the worldviews created by their discipline through exposing them to its language, methodology, and basic findings. Knowledge objectives were emphasized under the assumption that if uninterested students acquired some information, their sensitivity to and liking for the discipline would be enhanced (Kuhn, 1970).

Knowledge objectives were also favored because of practical reasons related to ease of presentation and documentation. The underlying problem here is lack of time, which has been identified as a primary concern in surveys of community college instructors (Garrison, 1967; Kurth and Mills, 1968). Bits of information lend themselves readily to straightforward oral or written presentation in traditional lectures, audiovisuals, and texts. Similarly, for purposes of assessment, bits of information were amenable to easy-to-construct objective, machine-scorable test formats. In contrast, if instructors had had higher cognitive objectives, they would have had to construct more difficult objective test items, which are time-consuming to write and require considerable expertise in test construction, or thought-provoking essay questions, which are difficult to grade and involve a large time allocation.

Furthermore, some instructors shied away from delineating and assessing affective objectives (despite their stated goal of interesting students in the subject matter) because of the "vagueness" surrounding them. As Bloom (1956, p. 7) noted, "Objectives in this domain are not stated very precisely; and, in fact, teachers do not appear to be very clear about the learning experiences which are appropriate to these objectives. It is difficult to describe the behaviors appropriate to these objectives since the internal or covert feelings and emotions are as significant for this domain as are the overt behavioral manifestations." By emphasizing knowledge objectives, instructors increased the efficiency of the instructional process in terms of objectives, methods, and assessment while accumulating concrete evidence of student "learning."

Another factor contributing to the development of knowledge objectives was the perceived lack of preparedness and motivation of students. For example, an accounting instructor said that in his ideal class he would have "students with firm background in business and extensive readers of all materials." In describing students as they actually were, he commented: "Students generally have low motivation . . . the principal problem is homework—that is, getting them to do it." When asked about student objectives for his course, he replied: "To get through it, since this course is required for any business degree."

This disappointment with students may be endemic among teachers in higher education. Cohen and Brawer (1982) cite increases in the number of ill-prepared students as a major factor contributing to faculty burnout. Logan and Van Fleet (1980) found that faculty members surveyed, teaching introductory courses at the University of Tennessee, unanimously attributed student failure to lack of personal concern, and a majority identified poor study habits and lack of high school preparation as contributing factors. Students, in contrast, attributed their failure to instructors' demands and attitudes.

By the time many students reach the community college, they are socialized into memorizing a body of information whether or not they find immediate use for it and whether or not it meets any of their needs other than obtaining a grade. Over time, collectively, these students exert an influence on instructors. For a variety of reasons, instructors and students may jointly "buy into" classes with low-level cognitive objectives, lectures, and objective tests. In fact, this type of class, which we have called the information-transfer course, was the typical class at Oakwood.

In Chapter Two, faculty perceptions of students' changing characteristics and their declining skills in reading and writing were reported at length. These changes in student motivations, attendance patterns, previous preparation, and literacy skills produced an evolutionary process through which instructors altered course objectives and expectations of student literacy behaviors away from the ideal as a way of coping with a changing clientele.

Instructor Coping

The response of faculty members to the perceived low literacy skills of their students was to reduce demands rather than to require students to improve skills. Instructors had few objectives directly related to reading and writing (except where language use or language learning was the central purpose of the course). This finding was buttressed by instructors' ratings of the relative importance of basic skills in five areas—reading, writing, listening, speaking, and math. Listening skills were considered more important than other basic skills. Only three rather low-level reading skills were viewed as having primary importance by the majority of faculty members interviewed, and most felt that developing habits of reading widely in their content areas or increasing interest in reading in general was not a primary concern for them. A similar pattern existed for writing. The only writing skill viewed as primary by the majority of instructors interviewed was taking lecture notes. Further, over three quarters of instructors felt that being able to organize an essay from an original outline was not important to them.

Reading and writing skill levels affected the choice of texts and the process of choosing them. Instructors reported spending increasingly more time in choosing texts, and those with lower reading levels were favored. They made a careful attempt to get student evaluations on textbooks. Despite faculty efforts, however, it appeared that textbooks were underutilized at Oakwood. An instructor in data processing reported that roughly two thirds of the students in classes he evaluated had said the book was too difficult to read. The campus bookstore supervisor stated that an introductory psychology text had sold very poorly. Of 4,000 copies ordered, only 180 had been sold. The bookstore supervisor also reported that many students resold their books and that they came back looking new.

Faculty members exhibited many innovative responses to the demands placed on them by poorly prepared students. Some developed essentially remedial course outlines or lab manuals that stressed material covered in lectures or in the text. Many reduced the amount of material covered or lowered their grading scales for tests covering reading materials. Very few faculty members outside English courses required composition writing. When instructors were asked whether they themselves imposed writing demands or whether they knew of any courses in which such demands were imposed, they were largely unable to identify courses that required any writing other than in multiple-choice exams.

One English instructor alluded to the direct effect of poorer preparation on methods of assessment:

> What's even more ludicrous, which I think you would agree, is: Here we are teaching about literature, and yet we permit them to write research papers on any subject that they choose. To me, there is such a dichotomy of thinking, if we would just say, "Okay, produce a paper only in the realm of literature"—you know why we stopped that? Because these students cannot handle it. We used to do this when I first came here. We were insistent that they wrote on literature. Write a research paper on literature. They cannot do it. They cannot.

This particular instructor adapted by requiring a two-page research paper on career plans in a course prerequisite to English literature:

> I guess I maintain that we should prepare them both for an appreciation of culture and for the world of work. So many of our students are terminal students. When in the realm of work will they ever need research papers? And yet, we make

a big thing of it in 102. I maintain it should be for information gathering. They should learn where sources are. They should learn how to evaluate these sources and then come to a conclusion about what they've learned. So, I get my digs in, in English 101. If they say to me, "I don't have a career, I'm just drifting," I say, "Fine. Find any career and do research."

It is, perhaps, in the area of testing that we saw the most pervasive adaptation by faculty members. Most instructors reported that exams had changed. In an extreme reaction, one instructor had done away with formal exams, feeling that most were glorified trivia exercises in which students simply crammed with the intention of forgetting later. Others preferred essay exams but, because of increased difficulties in simply reading students' writing, moved from essay to objective tests.

In commenting on why faculty members discarded writing assignments, an instructor remarked:

> Well, you can understand why, because if teachers have sixty to seventy students, when are they going to grade them? So they do the easiest thing. You look at any class that fills up with jocks, and you've got to be suspicious about what that teacher is teaching in relation to what he's demanding of his or her students. I mean this quite seriously. I'm talking about, you look at—I don't want to mention any particular department, but we who teach here know. And when certain classes start filling up with jocks, it's because no demands are made of them, and I'm talking about liberal arts classes, because word gets around. Believe me, word gets around.

Some instructors fashioned a rationale for deleting writing based on its lack of functional utility for students:

> How often will a person do actual writing in his career? When we really stop to think about it, how often is a person required to write in a demanding fashion when he leaves high school? Since

he hasn't been expected to write much in high
school, how many jobs require writing?

Most instructors felt it had been necessary to modify expectations; that is, they had become more "realistic" about
what students could be expected to accomplish in the class. Instructors noted that they were more prone to pitch the class
to a lower level of students. Initially, they had not worried
about the middle-to-lower half of the class but, rather, had
taught so that the upper third would be comfortable and middle students would have to reach to obtain the information. In
making adjustments to students with lower competencies, some
instructors felt, they were now boring their good students.

Instructors indicated that they went over the text in class
because the students could not handle it on their own. One
said, "I have to do a lot of remedial work as I teach course content. The ability level is down, so I must be more concrete and
less abstract in teaching."

Inspection of the number of activities that instructors
mentioned that they used to cover each objective substantiated
the prevalence of redundancy. Thus, instructors tended to have
low-level cognitive objectives and to provide two or more means
by which students could receive information.

Instructors' perceptions of students' poor academic preparation and poor attitude toward classes might have led them to
"crack down" on students for such behaviors as poor class attendance. College policies stated that instructors could drop students after three unexcused absences. However, very few instructors did this, for two reasons. First, they showed concern
for the students and took into account extenuating circumstances in their daily lives. Second, they were aware that retention data were kept on their classes, and they preferred not to
have a low rate of course completion.

Administrative pressures also influenced instructors'
adaptations of their course demands and expectations of students. Most instructors taught a fifteen-hour load per semester.
In social or natural science courses, assigning a writing task
meant facing over 125 papers to grade, assuming that one assignment was given in each class. Oakwood had an administra-

tive policy stating that assignments and tests were to be re-
turned promptly. "Prompt" was considered to be one or, at
most, two weeks' time. Thus, the labor involved also worked
against writing tasks. Beyond reading for content, had any faculty member corrected for composition, grammar, spelling, or
other basic skills, the task would have been enormous.

Faculty members complained of the lack of facilities
needed for effective instruction. For example, data processing
had less computer capacity than it needed. Classroom space was
also at a premium. Lack of phones and of someone to answer
them made it difficult for instructors involved intensively with
students, particularly in the English as a Second Language and
developmental areas. There was inadequate clerical and operations support. Instructors reported having to buy their own paper and do their own typing–if they could find a free typewriter.

Through their influence on teaching loads, operational
support, and the use of alternative teaching methods such as
television and audiovisuals, administrators contributed directly
and significantly to the decline in critical literacy in Oakwood
courses. Chapter Eight will discuss in greater depth the extent
of administrative influence on the decline of critical literacy in
the classrooms.

Student Skills and Instructor Objectives:
Reciprocal Effects

Institutional influences encouraging the use of different
instructional methods interacted with perceptions of the students' lack of motivation and knowledge. If students were unprepared, holding a discussion was viewed as futile. In using
instructional methods other than lecture, faculty members felt
thwarted by their students' low levels of preparation and enthusiasm. They were required to repeat coverage of materials,
and students asked few penetrating or exciting questions. Students lacking minimum levels of preparation slowed down instructors, making coverage of the skills and knowledge established as objectives problematic.

The perceived lack of student effort, however, probably

resulted in part from instructional methods and objectives. It was hard to imagine a typical student being kindled to great expenditures of effort in the class of an instructor lecturing and testing for low-level cognitive objectives when the material was also available in the textbook.

Because teachers saw students as representing a more diverse group than before, with a larger number being of "inferior" quality, they faced pressures to reduce literacy demands. Most did not see their teaching role as encompassing the development of basic skills. They considered themselves content specialists who identified with their disciplines. Trying to deal directly with literacy and language-related issues would have taken a great deal of work and time with little, if any, encouragement from peers or the administration.

In many community colleges, the resistance of instructors in most content areas to efforts to help students acquire or practice critical literacy—or instructors' lack of skills for participating in such efforts—has presented problems of coordination with the developmental and English skills classes that do exist. Students often cannot transfer skills from one context to the other and frequently complain that their skill work is irrelevant to their needs in other classes (Arwardy and Chafin, 1980). This situation has led to suggestions that content and developmental instructors work cooperatively to promote literacy. However, if instructors choose not to tackle the issue head-on through such efforts, they have to circumvent it. As a psychology instructor so aptly put it, "If they lower standards, then they are helping to perpetuate problems of incompetency. If they don't lower standards, then they can't reach many people. Teachers are in a bind."

This instructor's comment brings into focus the horns of the dilemma facing instructors. On the one hand, administrators and faculty members often thought of "good" instructors as those who adapted to their students' characteristics. If students studied less and had more trouble reading and writing, then shouldn't the "good" instructor find alternative ways of delivering content? This is what the psychology instructor was referring to when he talked about "reaching many people." On the other hand, "good" instructors were often thought of as being demanding but fair. If instructors did not make college students "text" in reading and writing, weren't they contributing to the "literacy problem" and to communitywide disappointment with a publicly supported institution where instructors allowed college students to "get by" with minimal development of written language skills?

Summary Discussion

Instructors' course objectives, then, had consequences for literacy in at least three ways. First, the absence of instructor objectives explicitly related to reading and writing created a paradox. Although instructors thought students should have adequate reading and writing skills, they did not take a frontal tack in dealing with perceived skill inadequacy. Specifically, by having only content-related objectives, instructors did not enhance student interest, habits, or skills related to reading and writing.

If instructors do not want to have course objectives related to reading and writing, then perhaps they could treat reading and writing as necessary enabling skills linked to successful completion of course objectives. Implementing this approach would require considerable consultation between instructors and instructional designers. Alternatively, students could be barred from entering transfer and occupational courses until their deficiencies in reading and writing had been remediated. In any event, if the college does not actively seek to foster the development of critical literacy, who will?

There was a second way in which the absence of objectives related to reading and writing in content courses affected the literacy behaviors observed at Oakwood. Teachers did expect students to read and write, but they did not comment on or grade student reading or writing. Consequently, students used reading and writing as they saw fit. Although social conventions existed calling for reading and writing in the classroom (for example, notetaking during a lecture), students were not evaluated on the process or product. Thus, students chose when and how they would use reading and writing, with little guidance from the instructor.

Reading and writing came to be seen as tools rather than as required competencies. The message sent by instructors was "You can get by without extensive or critical uses of written language." This point was underscored by students' view that the reading and writing they did were not "real" reading and writing.

Instructors could possibly increase the emphasis on critical literacy without, in turn, being overwhelmed by the resulting time demands. For instance, composing assignments might be copied and evaluated for writing problems by a learning assistance center or a writing lab. Again, developing solutions will probably entail pooling resources. We did not, however, observe any concerted efforts by faculty, staff, or administrators to deal with perceived reading and writing problems.

The third way in which course objectives influenced the nature of literacy involved the prevalence of low-level cognitive objectives involving isolable bits of information, which were usually covered by lectures and assessed by multiple-choice tests. Under such circumstances, it was not surprising that many students engaged in efficient strategies to "bit" their way through the courses.

The following description of an information disseminator, the modal type of instructor at Oakwood, illustrates the interaction among course objectives, teaching styles, and student behavior. The instructor, Ms. Flanders, described her approach to teaching in the following terms:

> I'm a straightforward lecturer. The amount
> of material and the newness of the material make it
> a hard course. . . . I give them study guides which
> are very detailed.

An observer described a typical class:

> The instructor turned her back on the class
> and wrote the first entry of today's lecture outline
> on the board. Then she returned to the lectern on

her desk and looked at us. Everyone got quiet and we were all ready to take notes. We wrote down what was on the board, and then the instructor began to lecture in her soft, soothing voice about diseases caused by certain microbes. She used the board often to write down more outline entries and to draw the structure of various microbes. She wrote the genus and species name of the microbes as she described them and what their functions were. Whatever she wrote or drew on the board the students put in their notes. This was all important information for the test coming up.

The instructor always stayed on the topic and very seldom even brought in personal references to illustrate a point. The few times she mentioned her family or a personal experience, it was a surprise but always relevant to the topic. The instructor very seldom asked students questions during the lecture. If she did, it was usually informal, and whoever knew the answer would blurt it out.

. . . She told them outright that the textbook was of "high reading level and difficult." She told them not to spend lots of time reading before they came to class, but afterwards. She said to skim the chapter, come to class, take notes, and then read the chapter. She also told students they didn't have to know so much chemistry. "Your textbook really gets into chemistry." Although she never directly told the students not to use the textbook, she did tell them, "I will never ask a question on a test that I haven't covered in class." She also said, "Your textbook is an aid."

The instructor also used a study guide, and when she handed it out, she said, "I can guarantee you that if you can answer these questions, you're going to pass the course, but your grade depends on how well you answer the questions." Throughout the semester, before a test, the instructor freely answered student questions on the study guide. She gave examples of test questions and what names to know and not know. She also explained various techniques for answering different types of questions.

The instructor's strategy for allowing students to succeed in her class included giving organized class lectures, writing notes on the board, telling explicitly her requirements and what she wanted them to know, giving a study guide over each unit, and going over each exam after it was graded. When the instructor saw that students were writing only what she did on the board, she adapted her own notes and made them much more complete. She also said it slowed her down so students could keep up.

Ms. Flanders was regarded by students and colleagues as an excellent instructor. She made certain that students learned the information basic to her discipline. She recognized that the text was too difficult for many of her students and provided alternatives in her lecture and a detailed study guide. The requirements for passing the course were clearly identified and did not involve in-class or out-of-class reading or writing not directly related to the bits of information specified. She delineated the nonessential from the essential, thereby minimizing the time required of students in meeting course requirements.

Over time, faculty members at Oakwood have come to view their students as possessing limited academic preparation and have adapted by preserving disciplinary content at the expense of literacy demands. They have preserved content by extensive cuing, by covering text material in class, and by constructing objective exams primarily testing knowledge-level objectives in the cognitive domain. They have adapted their requirements for reading and writing by reducing or eliminating the need for students to compose or read connected discourse. This mode of adaptation makes it clear that instructors at Oakwood contributed more to the problem of literacy than to its solutions. Before we judge them too harshly, however, it is important to consider the motivations of the students they faced each day, as well as the larger environment within which their classes were taught.

CHAPTER SIX

ళ్ళా ళ్ళా ళ్ళా

Student Motives
for Pursuing Education

ళ్ళా ళ్ళా ళ్ళా

The instructor's general disappointment with students and their adaptation to that disappointment through lowered expectations may have resulted from a conflict in beliefs, knowledge, and values concerning education. Students, as they interacted with their instructors, seemed to be operating under different basic assumptions about the purpose of higher education, the nature of the learning process, and the respective responsibilities of students and instructors (Morrill and Steffy, 1980). These assumptions influenced students' motives for participating in a course and underlay the strategies they adopted to meet the course demands imposed by instructors. In this chapter, we describe the motives of students and the view of education that those motives imply. We see this chapter as central to our discussion of literacy at Oakwood. The nature of student motives and the way the institution reinforced and responded to those motives was a key factor in explaining the lack of critical literacy.

In developing a framework for analyzing student motives, Houle (1961) identified three learning orientations of adults—learning-oriented, activity-oriented, and goal-oriented.

By "learning orientation" Houle meant the major conception that a person holds about the purposes and values of continuing education (p. 15). Boshier (1971, 1973, 1977) suggested that learning orientation may vary as a function of the types of educational experience and the nature of a particular learning environment. In adapting Houle's framework to an analysis of the motives of students at Oakwood, four major orientations emerged (Attinasi, Stahl, and Okun, 1982). Students interviewed about their reasons for taking particular courses were categorized, in most cases, as *requirement meeters, knowledge seekers, specific information users,* or *nonspecific information users.* Of course, other reasons were expressed, and many students voiced multiple motives for course participation. However, these four categories captured the range of motives discussed by Oakwood students. In addition, these motives could be linked with the students' participation styles in the classroom and their preferred uses of written language.

Four Orientations of Student Motives

Requirement Meeters. Requirement meeters were found in all classrooms at Oakwood and constituted the majority in the dominant, information-transfer class. The members of the attentive audience, quietly taking notes in lectures and skimming their textbooks in preparation for multiple-choice tests, were requirement meeters. Their strategies were adapted to the teaching of instructors who geared course activities to help students achieve rather narrow knowledge objectives.

The goal of requirement meeters was to obtain a good *grade,* or at least an accumulation of credit hours with passing grades. Students with this orientation were interested mainly in meeting course requirements as efficiently as possible.

> Just give me what I need to know. I'll go home and learn it. Then I'll come back and you can test me on it. Then I'll pass.

In addition to a pronounced focus on grades and credits,

requirement meeters were concerned about the amount of time that course work required.

> Question: What about the reading reports?
>
> I haven't started it yet. It won't be hard to do, but it is a waste of time. If it doesn't go for a test, it is a waste of time.

Students' concern about efficiency was reflected in their view of time as a commodity. In discussing time, students often used phrases with economic connotations, such as "spend time," "time is valuable," "time is precious," and "don't waste time." Requirement meeters chose study methods that allowed them to use their "time bank account" judiciously:

> The greatest grades I can come up with are a couple A's, a couple B's, a couple C's, just because there's not enough time. I've seen people that might just work weekends. Their grades are a lot better, but they have a lot more time to put into it. So, I do really well for the time I think I put into my classes.

Knowledge Seekers. In contrast to requirement meeters, a smaller percentage of students seemed to be knowledge seekers who were genuinely interested in the subject matter. They liked what they were learning and wanted to learn as much as possible.

> Question: Do you like lab?
>
> Yes, it is very interesting. I like looking through the microscopes even if it does make my eyes ache. It's neat when you see what she's been talking about. She'll describe something, and then you'll see, and say, "Eureka." I found I get those feelings sometimes.

Knowledge seekers, then, were intrinsically motivated students truly interested in learning the subject matter. As active participants who engaged in elaborate literacy strategies and took the student role seriously, knowledge seekers made their presence felt. However, knowledge seekers constituted a small minority. The class environment was negotiated around the needs of requirement meeters, so that knowledge seekers, over time, were actively discouraged from maintaining their unconventional (for Oakwood) motives.

Specific Information Users. Specific information users enrolled in courses because they expected to apply what they learned to some tangible and immediate objective, such as occupational advancement, job preparation, increasing the quality of their life, or doing better in other courses. Such students entered classes with a clear sense of what they were trying to achieve as well as the personal benefits they would receive. A specific information user commented:

> Now, I'm faced with having to go back to work to supplement our income, so I thought that I could at least brush up on my typing and maybe learn some other skills, enough that I could hopefully go into an office . . .

As this remark illustrates, specific information users were instrumental learners who viewed course work as a means to well-specified ends.

Although specific information users enrolled in a variety of courses, they were predominant in only one type, the small subset designated as vocational lab courses. Their motives were an appropriate match for the guide/resource orientation of instructors in these courses and the flexible, task-related activities they led. Students accepted a rather self-directed "worker" role because they recognized the importance of class activities to their own individual goals. These students used written language in highly selective ways; they read and wrote only when these tasks contributed to the objectives for which they had enrolled.

Nonspecific Information Users. Nonspecific information users were also motivated to take classes because of a perceived link to job procurement. By acquiring or improving basic skills, nonspecific information users hoped to improve their lot in life. In contrast to specific information users, however, they could neither judge whether their goals had been achieved nor describe how achieving their goals would lead to a better job.

At Oakwood, students with this motive were found within the most basic of the language skills classes, especially those designed for second-language speakers. When students in these classes were asked why they were enrolled, they typically said they wanted to learn English to get a better job, but they were unable to elaborate on any more specific aspects of this goal. When asked how they were progressing in the course, they simply said they didn't know because their instructor hadn't told them yet.

Because of their nonspecific objectives, these students readily took on the dependent role of obligatory respondents in the classroom and were open to the influence of the instructor's affective objectives. The reading and writing done by these students was limited to that carried out under the explicit direction of the instructor within the social context of the class sessions. The use of written language was not likely to arise in their own goal-directed strategies, because their goals were so vague and abstract.

Comparison of Motives

These four orientations can be compared along several dimensions. One dimension involves the outcomes that students sought in particular courses. For example, specific information users evaluated their success in terms of acquired knowledge and skills, which were subsequently applied to life, school, or work-related tasks. Presumably, by improving their performance in areas of course content, they enhanced their quality of life. Knowledge seekers, in contrast, evaluated their success in a class in terms of gratification received from the learning process. Requirement meeters, in evaluating their success, relied chiefly on the credits and grades achieved.

It was also possible to relate motives to Havighurst's (1976) ideas about the basic aspects of education. In Havighurst's scheme, instrumental education is education for a goal that lies outside and beyond the act of education. In this form, education is an instrument for changing the learner's situation. Expressive education, in contrast, is education for a goal that lies within the act of learning or is so closely related to it that the act of learning appears to be the goal. When Havighurst's concepts were superimposed on students' motives for taking courses, it was evident that students adopting a knowledge-seeker orientation were concerned mainly with the expressive aspects of education. Specific and nonspecific information users and requirement meeters were emphasizing the instrumental aspects of education.

Havighurst went on to point out that instrumental education is an investment of time and energy in the expectation of future gain, whereas expressive education is a consumption of time and energy for present gain. This notion helps to explain the relation we observed between student motives and time. Because knowledge seekers enjoyed the process of learning, they experienced immediate gratification. For specific information users, knowledge and skills had first to be learned and then applied. But since specific information users usually took courses of immediate interest, they typically experienced only a short-term delay in application.

For nonspecific information users, however, there was a long delay between learning something and applying it. Students often took several ESL courses without a clear sense of whether they were making progress. Their perceptions of success in school depended largely on the instructor's feedback. Nonspecific information users defined success in terms of being promoted by the instructor. This is, of course, precisely the situation in public schools and represents one of many parallels between Oakwood and public schools visible in basic skills classes. The connection between gains in basic skills and acquiring a better job seemed tenuous at best. For this reason, nonspecific information users experienced long-term delays in gratification.

Requirement meeters were task-oriented, doing just enough to obtain certain grades or to pass required courses. Because requirement meeters, like nonspecific information users, did not use the material they learned, except for passing tests, they had difficulty perceiving its relevance to other domains of their life (Knowles, 1978). They too experienced a long lag between acquisition and application.

Table 1 summarizes the characteristics associated with the four types of student motivations.

Table 1. Comparison of Motivational Orientations Along Three Dimensions.

| | Motivational Orientation | | | |
Dimension	Requirement Meeter	Specific Information User	Nonspecific Information User	Knowledge Seeker
Major criterion of success	Credit/ grade	Practical knowledge/ skill	Positive evaluation	Self-gratification
Aspect of education emphasized	Instrumental	Instrumental	Instrumental	Expressive
Time orientation regarding application of acquired skills/ knowledge	Long-term delay in application	Short-term delay in application	Long-term delay in application	Application *per se* irrelevant

Requirement Meeter as Modal Student

Requirement meeters were the modal type of student at Oakwood. Their preferences established the norms for classroom behavior. Requirement meeters branded as odd those students who expressed an interest in learning more than the minimum necessary to pass a course. Requirement meeters believed that students who participated and invested much time in a course were wasting time. They also deprecated students who asked questions they perceived to be off the task—that is, unrelated to exams:

But most of the questions the students ask aren't that important. Sometimes they're not even related to the book.

Question: Yeah, I've noticed that. Do you feel like those discussions are worthwhile?

Not really. They won't help you pass the class.

Both students and instructors seemed to value individuals by how they spent their time. Time was viewed by students and teachers alike as more important than innate ability in contributing to grade attainment. The "conspicuous spending" of time was evident in student interviews.

[Students] liked to talk of the many demands on their time for family, job, and so on. Students were bragging in a way. They were saying, "I can pass this course and do X, Y, and Z, too."

In a sense, requirement meeters derived status by spending as little time as possible on school-related matters. For example, Samantha explained as follows why she had done some problems that apparently few others in the class had: "It looked as though I was the only one who sort of knew what was going on, which probably wasn't true. It was just that I happened to have the time to work the problems." Similarly, Martin thought himself something of an oddity and virtually apologized for having the time to read: "Yeah, well, I read everything. I'm probably one of the few students who do. Well, I don't work, so I lead a pretty boring life."

The way in which requirement meeters were perceived by students with other motives was also interesting:

From the classes I've observed in the past, in this class so far people have not applied themselves totally to the class. . . . They are not behaving in a manner worthy of college students.

Question: What's a manner worthy of college students?

> Doing the book stuff and studies. Asking questions of the teacher, if I don't understand the information. Doing the lab assignments the best I can. . . .
>
> Basically, you have two groups—some who are here because they have to be here and some who are here because they want to be here. At this point, I could almost classify them name by name.

Covelli (1979, p. 36) compared today's community college students to "walkers" who "in making paths . . . find the most economical route to their destination." He argued that "students will choose the best routes if their educational destinations were clear and if there were ways to detect the most efficient and effective means of learning." Our observations suggested, however, that students sought an "economical route" not to learning but to course completion.

Eison (1981) showed that college students differ in attitudes toward grades. At one end of the continuum were grade-oriented students, whom we have called requirement meeters. At the other end were learning-oriented students, whom we have called knowledge seekers.

Each of these student types demonstrated a different type of literacy. Using our definition of literacy as the goal-directed use of reading and writing within the activities of a particular context, we can describe the literacy of the dominant student, the requirement meeter, as a noncritical literacy because written language was used in the absence of well-articulated educational goals. The students' goals were not educational in that they anticipated no specific gain in knowledge or skills but only the accumulation of credits and grades. Since their use of reading and writing was not guided by any need to understand and apply new learning, few, if any, opportunities were presented for the development of critical literacy.

Nonspecific information users also demonstrated a noncritical form of literacy connected to vague educational goals. Although these students did expect to gain skill and knowledge, they had little understanding of what that goal entailed. As a result, they did not develop independent literacy strategies but remained dependent on their instructors to direct their use of reading and writing.

Knowledge seekers and specific information users, in contrast, had the potential for developing critical literacy, but neither type was represented in significant numbers in most Oakwood classrooms. Each of these last two student types had clear educational goals in the sense that they were participating with the definite intent of acquiring knowledge and skills. In addition, each type had an understanding of what was entailed in acquiring their goals. As a result, both types tended to develop independent literacy strategies and used reading and writing in ways that demonstrated higher levels of thinking. Instructors, however, seldom reinforced or assisted these learners, concentrating instead on the requirement meeters or, in developmental classes, the nonspecific information users.

The contrast between the type of student who most influenced instructor adaptation and the students who did not is illustrated by the following description of two students in the microbiology course taught by Ms. Flanders, the instructor described in Chapter 5—Nancy, a typical requirement meeter, and David, a knowledge seeker and specific information user.

Nancy had purchased the textbook but said, "I haven't read the book. Do you know that I haven't even opened the book? Not the way she lectures; I don't feel I have to." Nancy did not read the lab manual, either; instead, she relied on the instructor's demonstrations and slides. "I like it because then I don't have to read the lab manual. It's faster and more to the point if she tells you what to do than if you sit down and read through this book on it." Nancy did read and use the handouts that the instructor said were important, and Nancy felt that notetaking was essential. However, she was very upset by having to write reports on technical journals. "I think it's a waste of time. I mean, if we were going to get some kind of grade on them, you don't mind spending the time if it's going to be to your benefit; someday you may want to read these things. But my time is limited. And I'm not going to get a grade. I would rather not waste my time coming to the library to look up some article."

In contrast, *David* read the textbook although the instructor told the class that tests would include only what had been covered in lectures. He said her lecture materials were easy, but he "liked to look at the book more." David felt the handouts were important, and he used them extensively. David, like Nancy, saw notetaking as an essential activity, but he added much extra material to the instructor's outlines. "I just put things down for my own, you know. Because later on in my own field, it'll come back." David related the class information to his chosen field on his own, and although he was not "thrilled with" the technical-journal assignment, he did not complain about it.

David's reaction to lab was "We've got to know that stuff," and he was glad to be learning it. David became very upset when the instructor, in response to one of his questions, said, "Someone's been reading the text." He was hurt because he felt she was disparaging him as a show-off; he said, "I sincerely wanted to know."

Summary Discussion

Students in Oakwood classrooms were given little opportunity to develop the critical literacy associated with texting. Instead, they practiced a type of literacy we have termed instrumental bitting. They did read and write but dealt only with fragments or bits of language and were given considerable assistance in understanding the meaning of the language that was used. They did not read extensively and were seldom called on to write more than a few words of connected language. Given the motives of students and the course objectives of instructors, the absence of elaborate or independent writing seemed predictable.

Written language, considered a tool by both students and instructors, was strongly influenced by the general characteristics of the teaching/learning process in Oakwood classrooms. Use of written language by students as requirement meeters was limited to that minimally needed to "get by." Those requirements, in turn, were set by instructors who possessed low-level knowledge objectives. Knowledge objectives led to a focus on isolable bits of information. The transfer of these bits defined teaching in these classrooms, while the ability to recognize the bits constituted learning.

Instructors built their teaching around knowledge objectives for a number of reasons, including their disciplinary commitment, their desire to carry out their teaching duties with a minimal expenditure of time, their disappointment with the ability of students to handle higher-level objectives, and their desire to maintain student accountability for course content.

Although exceptions did exist, these special cases did not alter the overall picture of literacy at Oakwood. A few knowledge seekers with articulated educational goals and stronger identification with the role of college student were present in every class, and these students did engage in more extensive reading and writing. However, as a small minority, they were viewed as oddities by the more numerous requirement meeters. Over time, they seemed to adapt to the norm of requirement meeting and instrumental bitting.

In some lab-oriented vocational classes, students had a more proactive, self-directed learning style aimed at acquiring specific job-related information and skills for which they saw a definite need. Students in vocational lab courses used written language selectively and only when it contributed to specific job-related goals. These classes were not numerous and seemed to represent a special case.

In some basic language skills courses, the mastering of language skills was often students' primary reason for enrollment. However, their level of understanding about the process of accomplishing their goals, as well as unfamiliarity with the college environment, put them in the dependent position of relying on direction from their instructors. Basic skills instructors, though ostensibly reading and writing teachers, seemed more oriented toward inculcating appropriate attitudes and behaviors in their students. Learning to read and write became essentially learning a set of classroom behaviors or procedures, and the written language involved was still limited to bits and pieces of disconnected discourse, processed in a highly structured social setting.

The typical classroom environments at Oakwood were actively hostile to students whose motives emphasized knowledge seeking or information using. The student and instructor roles have apparently evolved so that different performance expectations now exist. As instructors have adopted low-level cognitive objectives for their courses, they have relinquished requirements involving critical reading and writing. This change in focus has facilitated the emergence of the efficient student role in which students use instrumental bitting and other time-saving strategies to preserve as much time as possible for non-school-related facets of their lives.

Observation of the same students in different classes revealed that at least some students varied in their motives across classes. This suggests that instructors may be able to influence the kinds of reading and writing that students do. We are uncertain whether instructors did not encourage more critical literacy because they did not know how or because they did not want to expend the effort required.

This chapter has outlined the student motives that contributed to the emergence of dominant styles for teaching and learning in Oakwood classrooms. The requirement-meeter orientation of students was reinforced outside the classroom in their interactions during administrative tasks and in seeking support services. In the next chapter, we describe these nonclassroom activities and discuss the lack of critical literacy throughout the campus.

CHAPTER SEVEN

cℱₒ cℱₒ cℱₒ

Nonclassroom Influences on Literacy

cℱₒ cℱₒ cℱₒ

The out-of-class environment at Oakwood contributed to the lack of critical literacy in several ways. First, reading and writing activities of students throughout the college reflected instrumental bitting as the norm for written language. Although written materials were abundant, students' use of them was minimal and was heavily supported by oral communication. Second, students' experience at Oakwood reinforced the priorities of efficient requirement meeters who had little intrinsic interest in developing critical literacy skills. Students were not helped to plan comprehensive programs of study, nor were they oriented to the college and their role as students. There was a collegewide emphasis on maximizing student enrollments in individual courses rather than on helping students develop programs of study leading to graduation. Contacts between students and college staff members, like classroom interaction, focused on the communication of bits of information to meet college requirements.

Third, the institution did little to establish or maintain explicit standards of literacy. Slight attention was given to written language skills when students entered the college, when they participated in courses, or when they completed degrees. They had little incentive to develop reading and writing competencies, and only token assistance was provided to help them do so. Special programs and services, established to deal with nontraditional students, were expected to handle literacy-related problems, but such a limited solution to a pervasive problem proved to be inadequate.

Prevalence of Written Language

Written documents were ubiquitous on campus, and reading and writing were embedded in activities related to entering the institution and using its services. Oakwood produced 150 printed documents for students' use. Some were designed to inform students of college services, such as the learning assistance center or the veterans' affairs office. Others, such as the catalogue and the schedule of classes, provided information on college requirements and offerings. Approximately half were forms that required some reading and writing of information. Some forms were designed at a national level, such as the student financial aid form or applications for veterans' benefits; others were designed by the college offices for their own recordkeeping purposes, including requests for transcripts and applications for tutorial assistance.

Applying for admission, a student's first contact with the college, could involve as many as twenty-three printed documents. These included forms and handouts explaining procedures and directed toward applicants requiring special instructions, such as out-of-state applicants, international students, military personnel, students still completing high school, or college athletes. One program, nursing, required an additional eleven-page application form. As students went through the registration process, they were expected to make use of the college catalogue, the schedule of classes, and numerous forms and procedural notices. When students applied through the student financial aid office for a variety of grants, they encountered many of the thirty-three documents distributed by that office.

A Literacy of Dependence. The apparent importance of

written language was somewhat deceptive, however. As in class-rooms, many of the documents available were used in a cursory fashion if at all, and such use as existed involved the transfer of specific "bits" of information rather than the exchange of more extended messages. On forms, students were asked to fill in blanks with specific facts about themselves and their participation at Oakwood. The application form, for example, called for 34 segments of information covering a wide spectrum of personal data. The two forms requested for financial aid involved over 150 discrete pieces of information.

Written documents were seldom relied on to communicate more extensive information without significant use of oral language. Several factors contributed to the lack of independent use of written sources. The language in important documents was often too difficult for most students to comprehend independently, and the information requested was subject to multiple and changing interpretations. In addition, oral language was readily available and was built into required administrative tasks. For these and other reasons, Oakwood students increasingly used oral language in informal exchanges as an alternative to more extensive use of available publications.

Speaking and listening were increasingly important as student uncertainty became more pronounced. The technical directions on the financial aid application, for example, commonly left students uncertain about the requirements and, therefore, likely to ask questions about how to complete the task. For all students, "asking the right question" was critical. This was as true for students who did not have difficulty with reading and writing as it was for those who did. However, it was never clear how students learned to ask relevant questions. Students who had not expected to attend college and who did not have friends or family to help them were not as likely to be able to formulate appropriate questions.

Nontraditional students who persisted generally obtained assistance. In fact, some student services were established specifically to assist them or simply to do difficult tasks for them. It was not uncommon for students to take the form or paperwork of one service to another service for assistance. Such new offices as Chicano services and special services ended up assuming reading and writing responsibilities for their clients. Chicano services, for example, was frequently used by Spanish-speaking students to obtain assistance in completing the admissions application and the application for financial aid. Even as their English improved, these students continued to seek assistance from this office with many types of procedural questions.

The absence of orientation procedures and other clear, accessible channels to teach students college procedures, as well as the existence of special services to provide support, created dependence rather than developing the social competencies that students need to cope with either the college or the external environment. Of course, it is easier and more efficient to provide specific directions than to help people develop the skills to be self-directing.

The College Catalogue. The way the college catalogue was used illustrates the role that written materials played outside the classroom at Oakwood. Students who sought assistance with administrative tasks or other institutional procedures were frequently referred to the college catalogue. The catalogue, described as the "institutional bible" because it provided the official statement of policy, was perceived by staff, students, and faculty alike as the most important college document. The catalogue was divided into thirds. The first part gave an overview of the college, the second reviewed the curriculum, and the third part briefly described each of the courses.

Faculty and staff members, while commenting on the importance of the catalogue, often added, "But students don't read it." For a number of reasons, the catalogue was difficult to read and was not very useful as an independent source of information. It was described as vague, incomplete, disorganized, and poorly written. A readability analysis found that it was written at a relatively sophisticated level, averaging above the fifteenth-grade level. The catalogue exhibited considerable stylistic variation, reliance on technical vocabulary, and the use of compressed language with a high density of information. These stylistic characteristics required a highly mature and sophisticated reading ability not possessed by many of the students.

Actually, the characteristics of the catalogue were not surprising, because much of it was written with a concern for legal and procedural matters rather than with the objective of communicating to students. The section on the common core of the curriculum used legal terminology to establish the college's position on such policies as residency, veterans' regulations, and student rights. Some sections of the final version had been proofread by legal counsel rather than by anyone concerned with education. Course descriptions were produced at the district level and were common to all colleges. Hence, the primary criterion for wording many course descriptions was whether the language was parallel to that describing related courses at transfer institutions, not whether students could understand it. Although all students reported using the catalogue, they also reported using informal and/or oral means of gaining the same information. The catalogue as an institutionally constructed tool was necessarily enhanced and interpreted through direct, face-to-face interaction with friends, student services staff members, or instructors.

The catalogue, like most written materials at Oakwood, had evolved into a highly specialized tool that had to be interpreted for students. This development was similar to changes in the classrooms, where students were not expected to read textbooks independently or to compose connected discourse. Because available written materials could not be used without assistance in either setting, students became increasingly dependent on staff members, instructors, and tutors, who served in the role of modern-day "scribes."

Lack of Advisement

The instrumental bitting that characterized literacy at Oakwood was also reflected in the advising process, which focused narrowly on getting the maximum number of students enrolled in courses as efficiently as possible. This emphasis on efficiency in contacts with students contributed to the students' own focus on individual courses as well as their lack of program completion. In addition, the push to get students into courses, along with the lack of concern for degree completion (or even course completion), contributed to the faculty's focus on low-level cognitive objectives and unwillingness to invest time in working with students outside class.

Written materials and services reflected a lack of concern with degree completion. Administrators were more interested in the accuracy of sections of the catalogue dealing with legal requirements than of those focusing on program. The class schedule reflected limited attention to arranging classes so that full-time students could complete degree requirements without delays or substitutions. How much student objectives and institutional practices each contributed to the low graduation rate was not clear.

Beginning with the students' initial contact with the college, there was little evidence that they received advisement that would foster the planning of overall programs of study or long-term educational goals. In addition, the minimal nature of the students' contact with the institution did little to foster any sort of student culture or identification with the institution or the traditional college student role. Students were merely helped to enroll in classes. Once there, they naturally adopted an orientation toward completing the course—meeting its requirements. Little turned them toward larger goals related to an overall program or a commitment to being an intellectually curious college student.

If Oakwood had been as concerned with program completion as with efficient enrollment, the registration process would have incorporated more emphasis on orientation and advisement. Over time, however, the process came to focus solely on efficient course enrollment. Most new students arrived on campus, saw a line entering the registration site, and stood in it. After some frustrating encounters with forms and multistep procedures, they were enrolled in a set of courses. The nominal orientation, advisement, and placement that occurred as part of registration served primarily to expedite the flow of students into courses.

Orientation. Orientation had been an important service when Oakwood opened in the middle sixties. Three-hour orientation sessions were available throughout the summer. These sessions featured information sessions for large groups, followed by small-group sessions where students posed questions as well as received assistance in drafting their programs of study. As the number of students increased and more enrolled for part-time study, orientation sessions became briefer and less comprehensive. By the time of our study, the original three-hour time allocation had been reduced to fifteen minutes. The emphasis had also changed from helping students learn the college system to informing them about the registration process and course selection. The number of sessions had increased, but both the time allotted to each session and the content encompassed had been substantially narrowed. Once considered important enough to require a team of counselors, conducting orientation had become an assignment for work-study students.

Orientation sessions typically focused on a description of the procedures required for registration. The process was explained in detail, using overhead transparencies to illustrate the movement from place to place, the locations of faculty advisers and class cards, and other features of the process. The catalogue and the schedule of classes were described. Students were given instructions on how to complete their schedules, with special attention to avoiding conflicts.

Both students and faculty members agreed that orientation was not a priority of the college. Future plans involved elimination of any form of orientation other than a brief videotape presentation, owing to lack of staff and money. Since most students did not come with a well-developed understanding of why they were at Oakwood or how to utilize the system, this decreasing emphasis on effective orientation seemed to be unwarranted and undesirable.

Advisement. Academic advisement was also geared toward helping students select classes rather than plan programs of study. Advisement sheets identifying required courses were available for each of the college degree programs. Many students, however, did not complete this form until just before graduation, and 90 percent never reached that point. Many faculty members responded only to questions about courses in their own department. Hence, a student trying to design a program might be referred to a number of departments without ever finding anyone who understood, and could assist with, a degree-oriented objective. In addition, some faculty members used advisement as an opportunity to recruit students for their own courses.

The following descriptions of the registration process illustrate the lack of attention to advisement:

> I showed my completed schedule to the adviser. He had no questions; he just indicated that I needed to check the overhead screens for closed sections. I followed his advice, found sections that I wanted to take were closed, and made a new schedule of classes. Upon my return to the table, I showed the same adviser a new schedule determined by the courses that were not closed. He asked if they were all open. Upon an affirmative answer, he told me, "You better get your class cards quick."

> I told the adviser that I had never been to college before and didn't know what I wanted to take but I thought I was interested in nursing. She said she knew just the course that would be good for me. After describing the course, she said she was teaching it. . . . I asked if I didn't have to take an English course first, but she said, "No, not now." She said this course was really good because then I would find out if that was really what I wanted to study.

The objectives that students had made some difference in the type of advising they received. Transfer students frequently had not identified their upper-division majors and hence were viewed as no one's responsibility. Most faculty members teaching transfer courses advised few students. Transfer students were likely to seek assistance from other sources, including counselors, the catalogue, or transfer institutions. At the opposite end of the continuum were developmental students, who received considerable assistance from their instructors as well as from Chicano services and special services. In the middle range were occupational students, who were often advised in course settings by their instructors.

Faculty members were not unaware of the problems that students experienced when seeking academic advising. Most felt the registration process provided inadequate assistance. Some were concerned about the amount of misinformation students received because of the lack of an effective advising system as well as the many alternative sources of information students were likely to encounter as they sought assistance from such sources. Although instructors complained about this situation, they were generally unwilling to devote extra time to advising.

The evolution of faculty advising during orientation from a concern with program completion to an exercise in efficient course sectioning did not occur without some attempts to reverse this direction. In 1979 a proposal was written to design a system that provided advisers in "clusters" of departments, with an express table for students who did not need advising. A core of thirty faculty advisers selected for competence and commitment carried most of the student load. To free faculty members to function as advisers, work-study students assumed responsibility for procedural tasks such as class card distribution. A half-day session was held to acquaint advisers with their advisement responsibilities. Provisions were made for faculty, student, and administrative evaluation of all phases of the new procedures, and a tracking system was developed to evaluate the retention of students who had been through this advisement process.

Evaluations of the changes by faculty advisers participating were favorable; 73 percent indicated that they would voluntarily serve as permanent advisers in the future. Administrative evaluations were also supportive, and student evaluations were generally favorable. The results of the follow-up study on student retention were good as well. The data on student withdrawal generally indicated that advised students, whether day or evening students, had a substantially lower withdrawal rate than students who had not been advised.

From the evaluation, it appeared that the committee's efforts were highly successful and that the institution would adopt the new registration procedures. Armed with these results, the committee proceeded to make modifications for the January registration of new students and considered such steps as instituting advisement and registration for continuing students, changing the drop/add process, and establishing a permanent assignment of students to advisers.

However, the changes brought complaints from faculty members, producing, by spring registration, a compromise whereby more students were advised and the time period decreased. Objections by some instructors because they were working registration during a time when others were not accountable to the institution resulted in a decision that all instructors would work registration, which caused further resentment.

After the following fall registration, the committee's strongest supporter in the administration left the campus. Faculty complaints again surfaced. In addition to concerns about how many faculty members would work registration, there were complaints about training for faculty advisers, about advising in a cluster rather than advising by departments, about having student workers rather than faculty members pass out class cards, and generally about the long hours required to register and advise students by the new process. These complaints continued throughout the year. Eventually the faculty pressure resulted in a reversion to procedures in use before the 1979 proposal was written.

Thus, even a reform movement did not interrupt the trend toward *reducing the time commitments of full-time faculty members to increasing numbers of students.* In fact, the process of adapting student services to the circumstances created by a part-time student body and larger numbers of adjunct faculty members bore more than a passing resemblance to some of the changes observed in the classroom.

Frustrated in the attempt to reform the registration and advisement process, the advisement and registration committee turned its attention to the college catalogue as the most important source of information. Eventually the committee's work led to the development of an adviser's handbook and a revised catalogue with greatly expanded sections on advisement. In effect, the committee focused on developing improved written materials, in preference to continuing to try to change the behavior of their colleagues, an objective that appeared out of reach. Like most simple solutions to complex problems, the new handbook and the revised catalogue were better suited to dealing with symptoms than with the basic problems.

Placement of Entering Students

The deficiencies of the advising system contributed to the problems Oakwood experienced in assessing the reading, writing, and numeracy skills of entering students and placing these students in appropriate classes. Assigning students with widely differing language skills to the same class placed pressure on instructors to reduce demands on students and thus contributed directly to the process through which traditional forms of reading and writing were deemphasized in order to preserve content and to achieve acceptable retention rates.

Like most colleges, Oakwood required two courses in English composition of all students seeking a degree. However, for the majority of students who attended part-time the English requirement could be bypassed. Instructors in most courses therefore ended up dealing with a large percentage of students whose competence in language skills was unknown.

Added to the problems of those who bypassed the English requirement was the uncertainty associated with initial placement in English courses even for those who chose to enter composition courses. Except for the short-lived reform efforts of the advisement and registration committee during 1979-80, there was no placement process effective enough to identify reliably the students who needed instruction in basic skills. The screening procedures temporarily established by the committee illustrate the complexities involved.

In 1979-80 all full-time students and students taking an English course were required to complete a student planning sheet and a self-assessment scale, as well as a placement examination. The results of the placement exam were used to determine whether students should be admitted to one of three levels of remedial English or to the standard college composition course. For students whose placement scores indicated they should enroll in the basic studies program, an additional diagnostic procedure was established.

The abandonment of this revised registration process in 1981 reduced the effectiveness of the English placement process. Students needing help with writing skills were able to enter regular courses without being identified. Furthermore, instructors did not have data from assessment measures in such related skill areas as reading, oral language, or reasoning.

As instructors encountered the realities of extreme heterogeneity in entering students, courses at successively lower levels were established. English as a Second Language was added to the sequence. By the time this study began, a student could have taken two full years of remedial work at Oakwood without ever qualifying for admission to the first course of any regular degree program. Standards for progress also became an issue as the inadequacies of the remedial approach surfaced. Many students resisted placement in remedial offerings because they perceived the course emphasis as unrelated to their objectives, while those who wanted and needed remediation found themselves in large classes (twenty-five to thirty learners). Fewer than a third of those completing remedial sequences persisted into advanced courses, and a sizable percentage of those who did lacked the skills to complete the required work.

Faced with growing evidence that the objectives of remedial courses were not being achieved, Oakwood initiated the adult basic skills program. Although the program did offer an integrated format and special support services, its most unusual aspect was the change in objectives for students. For the first time success did not depend solely on performance in advanced courses. In fact, students enrolled in adult basic skills were not regarded as candidates for standard degree programs at all except under very unusual circumstances. Thus, the basic skills program was established as a separate and almost self-contained program with goals unrelated to regular college programs or standard forms of college literacy.

Special Services for Nontraditional Students

Student services at Oakwood experienced pressures for change similar to those operating within the classrooms. Increasingly, those entering Oakwood were from minority backgrounds, were the first in their families to go to college, lacked traditional academic preparation, and came with objectives that set them apart from the earlier clientele. These differences required adaptation from many Oakwood services designed around the needs of a less diverse student body. Members of the Oakwood support staff were no more enthusiastic about change than their faculty counterparts. If anything, they resisted the modification of their practices even more tenaciously because they lacked the subject matter refuge of the faculty. The result of changing needs and staff resistance was the establishment of several new services. The most important of these services were the learning assistance center, Chicano services, and special services.

Special programs or services designed to mediate between the needs of nontraditional clients and standard institutional programs and services served a stopgap purpose. The institution, faced with the need to change existing services and programs or add new ones, elected the latter as the less complex solution. The hope was that a buffer would be created between students and the traditional services, which would be left to carry on business as usual. Although some instructors initially voiced philosophical disagreement with the existence of special programs, they generally came to accept them, hoping their own classrooms would remain relatively free from the problems these services were designed to address. From the institution's perspective, the decision to create special programs and services was made almost irresistible by the actions of external agencies, including the federal government, in providing grants to fund them.

Special programs and services provided the time and resources necessary for gradual accommodation, preventing the conflict and institutional trauma that might have resulted from an attempt to adjust more quickly to changing characteristics of students and evolving conceptions of educational mission. However, the decision to establish a new program or service was, at the same time, a recognition of the inadequacies of existing programs and services.

The Learning Assistance Center. The learning assistance center (LAC) was established as a division of the library to provide tutorial assistance to students having difficulty with course work. The greatest demand was for tutors in basic math, reading, and English courses. Within two years, the demand for services tripled. During its heaviest month in 1979–80, the LAC furnished 340 students with almost 2,400 hours of tutoring.

Because it provided individualized assistance to students, the LAC was also a support mechanism for the faculty. Rather than having to spend more time with the increasing number of students they often described as underprepared, faculty members were able to refer them for assistance. Thus, an important justification for the LAC was the inability of instructors to teach some students successfully within the constraints of the classroom. From this perspective, it was clear that the LAC represented an important adaptive strategy for coping with increasing numbers of students who needed assistance in meeting the academic requirements of the college.

Chicano Services. Another of the new services at Oakwood was a special office for Chicano students. Originally established to assist the college in recruitment, the Office of Chicano Services had as its stated purpose to promote education in the Hispanic community and to assist individuals in the development of their educational goals. The office had two major functions: outreach and on-campus services. Outreach activities included contacting local high schools, encouraging potential students to attend, and working with community agencies. On-campus services included financial aid information, admissions and records information, and referral to other services and non-campus agencies, as well as providing institutional information, job referrals, and transfer information for Chicano students.

Chicano services provided incentive for Chicanos, especially those with limited English-speaking skills, to take advantage of the "open door." Many Chicano students received initial information about the college from Chicano services as well as assistance in applying for admission. They continued to use the service after enrollment. Students who had not been recruited through Chicano services often heard about it from their friends or from the Chicano student club on campus.

Chicano services provided a support system for Hispanic students, many of whom lacked prior academic preparation. The important factors that contributed to the effectiveness of Chicano services were language, informality, direct assistance with forms, and referrals to other services or community agencies. Some students lacked the English language skills required to complete forms, and special attention was given to assisting them with the admissions and financial aid applications. For many students, Chicano services was a place where they could find a friendly, brown face or a compadre. Students in the intensive English for Spanish Speakers program, who spoke little English, described Chicano services as a central place where they were able to find someone willing to talk with them in their own language.

Special Services. Following the establishment of Chicano services, a proposal was written requesting federal funding for a special services program to assist students by providing support and instructional services for handicapped, limited-English-speaking, and low-income students. The Office of Special Services also assumed responsibility for the advisement of international students. Although this program continued to receive support from federal funds, over time the director and one counselor were transferred to the college budget.

Services provided to eligible students included testing by referral to the testing center, development of an educational plan, development of a class schedule for each semester, and continuing contact related to specific student needs. Special services also provided some support for tutors at the learning assistance center when eligible students were referred.

Handicapped students sought assistance with mobility problems. Limited-English-speaking students used the office as a comfortable place to bring their questions and saw staff members as individuals to whom they could relate. In addition to requests for assistance with academic advisement, students brought concerns about grades, transportation, housing, and college-related procedural matters.

In some ways, special services and Chicano services were competitors. When Chicano services was established, it was staffed by paraprofessionals who knew the language and were familiar with the communities where their clients lived. Almost from the beginning, responsibilities for recruiting were matched by efforts by Chicano services to make traditional Oakwood services responsive to the students whom recruiting produced. The traditional services, however, were staffed by professionals who saw the emergence of Chicano services as an implied criticism of their ability to work with nontraditional students. The professionals especially resented the suggestion that their actions should in any way be guided by the suggestions or preferences of Chicano services staff members, whom they saw as lacking the professional training that would have permitted their treatment as equals.

Thus, special services was an attempt to establish an alternative to Chicano services, staffed with professionals who would be more acceptable to the professionals staffing traditional student services as well as to the faculty. In addition, there was the perceived need to respond to handicapped students and others needing special assistance besides Hispanics. Although the staff included a Spanish-speaking professional counselor, the service never became the home away from home that Chicano services represented for Spanish-speaking students. And when black students asked for their own service to provide equal attention to their needs, they did not see special services as the appropriate response.

Summary Discussion

Students did not need to read or write to be admitted to Oakwood, to register for classes, or to qualify for financial aid. In one extreme example, one of our researchers, who is bilingual, posed as an applicant and managed to register for classes and complete a financial aid form without speaking a word of English. After initial frustration, he eventually encountered a Spanish-speaking security guard who took him to Chicano services, where someone completed the writing requirements for him.

The classroom emphasis on requirement meeting found its counterpart in the single-minded focus on efficiency in enrolling students in discrete courses. Program completion was not a priority, as evident from observations of the advising process and reviews of the college catalogue and class schedule. Instructors recognized the shortcomings of all three, but most were unwilling to devote more of their own time to making improvements.

The influx of nontraditional students brought changes to such services as admissions, registration, and financial aid as well as pressures on the classroom. The orientation of services toward the use of oral communication made literacy skills less important but also made students more dependent on the staff in completing the administrative requirements for being a student.

Finally, new services were established for students considered to have special problems that interfered with access or progress. Chicano services would complete forms, interpret written instructions, and help students bypass or cope with more traditional services, such as financial aid and counseling, where there was more resistance to simplifying procedures for students who had difficulty reading and writing.

Oakwood also structured special programs and services to augment the efforts of the instructional programs in dealing with nontraditional students. Efforts to provide remedial courses at successively lower levels culminated in the establishment of a basic skills program, which accompanied efforts to improve very limited reading and writing skills with an emphasis on citizenship and socialization reminiscent of the self-contained classrooms of secondary schools in the sixties. A learning assistance center provided tutorial assistance in reading, writing, and mathematics to help students cope with the reduced literacy and numeracy demands of regular and remedial courses.

These remedial and developmental services kept the most

nontraditional students out of college-level courses. Very few students who entered remedial courses ever progressed into regular course offerings. Limited credit toward a degree for remedial work kept these students eligible for the financial aid they needed to stay in school.

Oakwood faced a series of paradoxes, which may have prevented the articulation of a literacy policy. Enrollments were required in order to maintain the financial base. Maintaining enrollments meant seeking and accepting students lacking in academic preparation and language skills. Permitting these students to enroll freely would have created worse teaching conditions. Nonetheless, because most of these nontraditional students needed financial assistance, courses in which they enrolled had to carry credit toward degrees to meet federal guidelines. Awarding credit toward degrees for noncollegiate courses contributed to a reduction in academic standards as well as concerns about credibility.

More important, the literacy problems at Oakwood could not be addressed effectively through special programs for special students. Instructors perceived the *majority* of their students as significantly different in skills and motivation from their notion of a competent college student. From their perspective, such students made teaching more difficult and less satisfying. The college environment and the institutional forces that shaped it, however, reinforced the motivations and learning strategies of requirement-meeter students and seemed to support instructors in their strategy of reducing language demands as the preferred way to cope with the new clientele. Certainly, little was done to encourage or assist faculty members in maintaining standards for critical literacy.

In the next chapter, we examine the indirect influence of administrative priorities and strategies on the literacy problem at Oakwood. Faced with needs for adaptation, Oakwood administrators changed what they felt they could and learned how to live with the rest. This examination of administrative strategies leads into a discussion in Chapter Nine of how Oakwood and similar open-access colleges might intervene to promote critical literacy.

CHAPTER EIGHT

❧ ❧ ❧

Impact of Administrative Priorities on Classroom Literacy

❧ ❧ ❧

During our study, Oakwood Community College expanded its educational mission and increased the size and diversity of its student population. Though resisted by significant numbers of faculty members and administrators, these changes had an impact on the educational program and the campus environment as a whole. The reading and writing expected of students in this institutional setting took on a form that we called bitting because it involved the use of bits of written language and a dependence on others to derive meaning from those bits. Because bitting did not involve skill in analyzing or evaluating information and because the students did not have well-articulated educational goals, they were not developing critical literacy skills. To understand why critical literacy was not maintained as an essential outcome of instruction at Oakwood, we now need to extend our analysis to examine external influences, institutional responses, and the impact of these contextual variables on student and faculty behavior in the classroom.

120

Administrative efforts to achieve or prevent changes in educational programs and services affect faculty and student attitudes by redefining institutional norms. Through use of communication nets and the resource allocation process, such efforts define the institutionally desired balance between serving all students at some minimum level or serving a more selected clientele at some higher level of definable outcomes. Administrative decisions affect class size, faculty work load, availability of learning aids, and the time requirements within which learning must occur. The web of administrative decisions and the methods of communicating and enforcing them contribute in a major way to the context within which literacy is defined in a community college.

To begin an analysis of administrative influence, we consider the decision-making process, the priorities that resulted, and the strategies used to promote those priorities. Then we examine the response to these priorities reflected in faculty and administrative commitment and the consequences for classroom literacy.

Decision Making and Priorities

Two primary influences governed decision making. The first was information, which was widely distributed among administrators. The contribution or withholding of information constituted the major or only influence of most administrators on decision making. The second was the allocation of resources, closely controlled by the chancellor. Because most decisions required resources for implementation, the use of discretionary resources to support priorities was an important strategy for change throughout the course of the study.

The complexity of the district, combined with the administrative structure of the colleges, resulted in a system of filters such that persons at the bottom or top of the organization received information that had been subject to multiple screenings. As one result, key administrators had limited information about students and the classroom setting. They knew head counts, full-time equivalencies, ethnic breakdowns, and class sizes. However, most were long removed from the classroom setting and had little information about how student characteristics affected the learning process. Classroom literacy was not a meaningful concept for most administrators.

Similarly, instructors received most of their information about district policy from other instructors who had read something or heard a rumor. Instructors reported that they interacted almost exclusively with instructors at their own campus. In consequence, their perceptions of decisions made by the chancellor almost always included some distortion of intent or content.

These circumstances provided fertile ground for conflict, misunderstanding, and frustration. They were particularly important in governing the expectations that administrators held for special efforts to affect literacy, such as developmental education. Almost without exception, there was a direct relation between administrators' distance from the classroom and their tendency to overestimate the results and underestimate the costs of such efforts, as well as to misjudge the indirect consequences of all policies for classroom literacy.

When the new chancellor assumed office in the fall of 1977, he found a highly centralized, single-college structure that discouraged initiative and responsibility among campus administrators while facilitating governing board intervention in administrative process. The practice of promoting administrators from within as a reward for faithful service, combined with the district's roots in a public school system, had produced an insular administration perceived to be out of touch with the mainstream of emerging community college emphasis on serving new clienteles. The educational program, though comprehensive, was university-oriented and highly traditional as the result of faculty preferences and a period of benign neglect from administrators. Faced with this situation, the incoming chancellor saw a need for change.

A planning process initiated in the fall of 1978 resulted in the identification of four priorities reflecting the chancellor's assessment of needed changes in educational programs and services. One priority, addressing fiscal constraints and a reduction in the pool of traditional students, focused on attracting greater numbers of nontraditional students. In an early speech to the faculty, to dramatize this priority, which was aimed at improving the district's financial base, the chancellor used the words "FTSEs [pronounced "footsies" and standing for *full-time student equivalents*] are the name of the game."

Added to this priority were three others, which received strong support from key administrators during the study. A second priority, for student retention, was added partly to address faculty concerns that the district was overemphasizing the recruitment of new students, relative to what it was doing for the ones already there. Of course, this priority also fit well with administrative concerns for maximizing enrollments in order to improve the fiscal base.

A third priority, developmental education, was the logical consequence of the decision to recruit students who lacked the literacy and numeracy skills to succeed in existing courses. To achieve this priority, the district established a Developmental Education Advisory Committee to complement campus task forces already operating. The chancellor also initiated a discretionary fund of $200,000, for which the individual colleges were encouraged to compete by submitting proposals. Significantly, during the 1979–80 academic year, virtually all the proposals funded were related to developmental education or student retention.

The fourth priority, which emerged during the spring of 1980, was occupational education. Beginning the next fall, the district, in rapid succession, created a new position, director of occupational education, staffed it, and then created a district task force that, by the fall of 1981, had developed—and secured board approval of—a five-year plan to strengthen occupational programs, including a first-year financial commitment of $5 million.

Each of these four priorities contributed in significant ways to changes in college literacy. The decision to recruit a new clientele brought to the campus more students with different objectives and skills than those traditionally served. The emphasis on retention and the preservation of attrition statistics placed pressure on instructors to avoid literacy demands that would have resulted in higher student attrition. The emphasis on developmental education and, in particular, the redefinition of the purposes of such courses to include objectives not directly related to academic achievement exerted pressure on instructors to continue the process of reexamining their own expectations for student reading and writing behavior. Finally, the concern with occupational education contributed to the trend we observed toward a functional, less "collegiate" definition of literacy.

District Strategies for Achieving Priorities

The process of achieving priorities involved defining goals and allocating resources. Many groups had input into this process, but the key decision to implement remained with the chancellor and his cabinet, providing a fail-safe mechanism for ensuring attention to their priorities. The strategies used by Richfield administrators to promote their priorities included reorganization and staffing changes, planning, resource allocation, and staff development.

During the early stages of the new chancellor's tenure, reorganization and staffing changes were emphasized, resulting in high levels of conflict. Following this period of intense conflict, key administrators made greater use of planning, resource allocation, and staff development to encourage voluntary commitment. As a consequence, the pace of change was slowed, resulting in moderation of the conflict as well as less focused pursuit of priorities.

Reorganization and Staffing. During the early part of the study, then, reorganization and related staffing changes were used to cause major change, with the effect of unfreezing the district from its previous traditional (by community college standards) posture. Structural changes included establishment of a college without walls and of a comprehensive college to address the special needs of minority students, as well as implementation of an extensive student recruiting process. Staffing changes included appointment of many outsiders to key district positions, creation of new positions, and appointment of special task forces in such areas as developmental education and occupational education.

One important effort that made use of the strategy of reorganization was the decentralization of decision making and budgetary responsibilities to give greater latitude to the college presidents. This decision was made by the chancellor, endorsed with varying degrees of enthusiasm by other key administrators, and implemented in stages over a two-year period even in the face of obvious fiscal problems. The importance attached to this strategy resulted from the chancellor's desire to have presidents buy into district priorities and assume a proactive role in their achievement. Under the previous centralized administration, the presidents, then titled executive deans, had served more in a caretaking and mediating role, with neither the discretion nor the resources to contribute to the achievement of district priorities to the extent desired by the new chancellor.

Presidents were not uniformly enthusiastic about the increased responsibilities they were asked to assume. Part of their restraint resulted from the perception that decentralization altered their responsibilities more significantly than it did their ability to influence resource allocation. Budgeting amounts requested invariably exceeded funds available. Expenditures in fixed areas such as district-mandated salary increases and utilities left little in the way of discretionary funds available to presidents. In one year, amounts allocated were less than increased obligations resulting from the salary settlement, despite a significant increase in the number of students attending.

The college presidents were further constrained by their inability to hire additional staff to carry out the new responsibilities. Invariably, staff members previously responsible for these functions remained at the district office and assumed new responsibilities. College administrators picked up the responsibilities in addition to their other duties. The result was an upgrading of salaries and titles for some college administrators, placing further pressure on the annual budgets. Despite these constraints, the selective decentralization of responsibilities seemed effective in encouraging colleges to give attention to district priorities for educational change.

Strategies involving reorganization and staffing changes

were relatively easy to implement. However, when they im-
pinged on issues of importance to the faculty, as did the forma-
tion of a college without walls, they brought prolonged conflict
and subsequent faculty resistance, on principle, to other new
administrative initiatives.

The practice of using adjunct faculty in staffing either
existing campuses or the new college without walls was one of
the most sensitive issues dividing administrators and the full-time
faculty in the Richfield District. From the district's perspective,
this was an economical and flexible procedure for expanding
services. From faculty members' perspective, it demeaned what
they did by proceeding from the assumption that anyone could
come in, throw together a few assignments, and be credited with
providing the same level of instructional services as the full-time
faculty. Through the use of part-time visiting staff, the district,
in the eyes of faculty members, undervalued them and their
efforts. The threat was perceived as financial, personal, and
professional.

The issue had important implications for the achievement
of district priorities at Oakwood. Theoretically, full-time faculty members could be given released time to participate in the
development of new efforts such as the basic skills program.
The courses left unstaffed by reductions in teaching loads
would then be covered by the much less costly adjuncts. Thus,
development of new programs and services required by the
changing student clientele could be accomplished by full-time
faculty members while being financed at less than the income
generated from their enrollments. In practice, most instructors
avoided the more difficult curriculum development or teaching
responsibilities even when provided with the additional induce-
ment of summer employment. Beyond refusing to participate,
they made life difficult for those who did, sometimes by open
criticism but more often by excluding them from the normal activities that marked collegial acceptance at Oakwood.

Planning and Resource Allocation. One of the most effective strategies for achieving attitudinal change about the importance of district priorities was the use of a formal planning process. Planning helped to reduce conflict by lengthening the lead

time necessary for implementing change and by establishing a wider range of formal goals more representative of the values of all faculty members and administrators within the district.

Within a year of his arrival in the Richfield District, the new chancellor implemented a planning process using a "charette concept" characterized by intensive activity in a marathon format. Representatives from across the district, designated as the Joint Council on Educational Priorities (JCEP), completed planning tasks under pressure of time, guided by a skilled group facilitator. Before the planning session, working papers and factual data had been prepared. The process resulted in fifteen goals representative of the interests of those who participated.

Broad-based task forces from across the district were then established to address individual priorities by undertaking detailed planning. Resources were allocated to achieve the objectives identified. Developmental education was the first priority tackled by this approach, but the process did not reach maturity until it was used to address occupational education during the 1980–81 year. Following the striking success of this group, the task-force approach was expanded to include groups focusing on arts and sciences and honor programs, two concerns that had emerged from the general faculty during the period of extensive attention to occupational education.

When the state legislature passed a bill in 1980 limiting the authority of local boards to levy property taxes, key administrators realized that simultaneous pursuit of all the goals identified through the JCEP planning process was unrealistic. By controlling the commitment of resources, key administrators were able to pursue preferred objectives even when resources were severely constrained. In one instance, the position of marketing director was created and staffed to head an effort to recruit new students while faculty and staff vacancies were frozen at the colleges to balance the budget. Key administrators also used discretionary funds to reduce the work loads of faculty members who were willing to "play ball" by working on projects related to district priorities.

Administrators also increased their level of control over the curriculum through a special planning project to standardize course offerings. Because responsibility for these courses had been delegated to the faculty by the previous administration, with little if any provision for accountability, course content varied widely on the different campuses for courses with the same district course-bank number. This variation was cited by universities as a partial justification for withholding credit toward degrees for some courses. Under the direction of the vice-chancellor for educational development, district instructional councils composed of faculty representatives from related disciplines devoted considerable effort to standardizing courses by specifying goals, objectives, content outlines, and evaluation methods. Although this strategy did place some limits on faculty autonomy to determine course objectives and content, full-time faculty members supported the project because of their concerns about the impact of the increasing numbers of adjunct faculty on program quality.

Staff Development. The importance of staff development as an administrative strategy following the climactic and conflict-laden year of 1978-79 was evident from the number of activities sponsored by the district in relation to high priorities. For 1979-80 student retention was high on the list for key administrators, and seven activities were carried out, reflecting such diverse concerns as analyzing teaching techniques, math anxiety and avoidance, needs of the vision- and hearing-impaired, and training developmental studies personnel.

Although most faculty members failed to attend any activity (the average attendance rate for Oakwood instructors in 1979-80 was only 14 percent), those who did participate found social support as well as new information to assist them in pursuing administrative priorities. For administrators, staff development activities constituted important evidence of progress toward achieving objectives. Even for nonparticipating faculty members, the activities suggested a changing order and raised the cost of overt resistance to the priorities the staff development sessions were organized to promote.

As would be expected from the preceding discussion, participation in staff development activities and support for district priorities were directly related. Instructors in math and social science were the most resistant to staff development activities, while those in the business and career programs were the most likely to participate. Interviews confirmed the greater impact of underprepared students on the departments with the lowest participation rates. These were also the departments whose instructors showed the greatest active resistance to district priorities.

Staff development activities were by no means limited to formal presentations or to instructors. At the district level, the chancellor implemented a modified management-by-objectives program, leading to an annual evaluation. The impact was to tie district administrators more securely to their responsibilities for achieving district priorities.

Administrative Strategies at Oakwood

The administrative strategies at Oakwood supported district priorities to the extent feasible given the set of implicit rules for change that prevailed on that campus. These rules were as follows: (1) Disregard a problem as long as possible. (This statement applied because of limited resources.) (2) Use an incremental approach when dealing with a problem identified as requiring attention. (For example, the learning assistance center was built on tutoring services, which were already known and accepted.) (3) Test the market; that is, consult carefully with instructors or anyone else who may be involved, but don't commit yourself. (4) Use existing staff whenever possible; don't bring outsiders in if you can find other ways to get the job done. (5) Don't evaluate. (6) Don't make plans for the maintenance of change. If something is worthwhile, it will continue.

Many of these rules contrasted sharply with the approach used by the district during 1978-79. The district was interested in significant changes, used many outside consultants, and attempted to identify problem areas and to deal with them aggressively. This placed severe pressure on Oakwood administrators, because they literally could not conform to district expectations and still maintain a cordial working relationship with the Oakwood faculty.

Signals emanating from the district office strongly influenced Oakwood administrative strategies. Most formal planning on the campus involved responding to district imperatives or dealing with circumstances that, if not already a crisis, seemed likely to become one. When the chancellor, under the auspices of the Joint Council on Educational Priorities, required individual colleges to produce plans responding to district objectives and assigned priorities, he placed a new burden on college administrators. Even though Oakwood produced a plan that complied with district expectations, Oakwood administrators perceived that the plan was never read by district administrators.

Priorities for Oakwood in responding to district objectives were determined mainly by the president and dean of instruction, who tested proposals with faculty members to ensure that they would not result in active resistance. One administrator summarized the process this way: "Faculty are involved in discussing objectives, but administrators determine priorities." Once priorities were established and available resources allocated, Oakwood administrators developed plans for implementation in their own areas of responsibility. Even where committees were not involved, there was always a lot of informal consultation with instructors. Ideas were tossed out for comment. Administrators described this process as cumbersome but workable. Interestingly, evaluation was seldom used as an administrative strategy, because Oakwood, like most community colleges, had little systematic evidence relating outcomes to objectives. According to one administrator, the college operated on the principle of evaluation used by Marshall Fields (a major department store): "If it sells and keeps on selling, we don't worry about it. If something goes well, we don't evaluate it for fear we'll find something wrong and have to stop offering it." In addition, formal evaluation requires time and staff. Administrators at Oakwood were simply too busy keeping the operation going to have any time to worry about activities perceived as nonessential.

Despite the absence of systematic and organized data on outcomes, administrators did engage in informal evaluation. Critiques were held in the administrative council and in the meetings of department chairs after important functions such as registration. The results of these discussions were used to improve procedures in subsequent cycles. Administrators also valued the information they obtained through informal talks with faculty members and students.

The lack of information about outcomes was related to the absence of defined objectives for most programs. The need to relate college goals for developmental students to the students' goals was recognized. However, no one was sure what the students' goals were. Assessments had not been completed before the developmental programs were designed. There was no research on why people left or why they stayed. In one section of the adult basic skills program, there was almost no attrition, but virtually none of the students achieved the instructor's goal of a fourth-grade reading level by the end of the course. It is possible that the absence of evaluation served a functional purpose, since neither administrators nor instructors were very optimistic about the college's ability to help low-level students. In fact, the objective of developmental programs most commonly emphasized by the dean was to keep underprepared students from taking up space or detracting from the learning environment in the transfer and technical courses. According to instructors, the developmental studies program had been effective in achieving this objective by keeping departments such as business, psychology, physics, and social science from being affected by lower-level students.

Administrative strategies were constrained by both internal and external factors. The level of staffing, as well as the experiences and value preferences of those in positions of responsibility, had an effect on administrative efforts to achieve change. When the new chancellor arrived, Oakwood was better prepared, by virtue of its administrative staff, to implement decisions reached elsewhere than to assume major responsibility for developing new initiatives. In addition, Oakwood administrators, with few exceptions, had come through the ranks of the faculty and shared faculty preferences for avoiding change unless the need and desired direction were clearly established. Ultimately, however, the most serious constraint was the inability to acquire additional resources at the college level to permit staffing and support of proposals for change.

Concern about the availability of resources dominated

decision making at Oakwood. Administrators encouraged instructors to be certain students did not drop out before the
sixth week of classes, when they were counted for state funding. Despite faculty comments, the problem was not absence of
essential materials. It was the prevailing perception, shared by
administrators and faculty, that the district adequately funded
only those changes linked to its highest priorities. The imbalance of students and resources was said by some faculty members and administrators to be growing steadily worse as a result
of recruiting. The perceived imbalance accounted for much of
the faculty and administrative resistance at Oakwood to recruiting and serving underprepared students. Some also wondered
about the future of new programs and services when outside
funding ceased.

The problem did not improve with the adoption of the
1980-81 budget. The budget for Oakwood increased by approximately 11 percent, but Richfield granted salary increases
in excess of 12 percent. As a consequence, Oakwood's requests
for additional personnel to help achieve programmatic priorities
and to compensate for increases in enrollment could not be
approved. For the 1980-81 year, Oakwood was staffed at about
the same level as the preceding year despite an enrollment increase exceeding 7 percent. The campus analysis of the budget
increase indicated that it would barely cover the salary increases. The president reported that it would be impossible to
hire new people and that a counselor placed on disability probably also would not be replaced. Additional evidence of growing
fiscal stress, resulting in part from legislative action to limit governing board taxing powers, was provided by the decision to ap-
point a committee to study the underfinancing of the library
and a commission to study the future of financing for the Richfield District.

Despite the growing disparity between objectives and
available resources, Oakwood was deeply involved in district
planning for facilities expansion. Expansion presented Oakwood
administrators with a dilemma. Their existing facilities were
overcrowded, and enrollment continued to grow. However, part
of Richfield's strategy to develop new facilities was the use of

funds generated by enrollment increases. Such funds could also have been used for additional staff and the improvement of services. Oakwood administrators supported both the development of new facilities and the improvement of services with the expectation that ultimately they would not be forced to choose between the two.

Additional income generated by increases in enrollment did not automatically flow to campus programs and services. After one particularly large increase in full-time equivalent students, a faculty representative on the Oakwood Administrative Council asked whether the increase would result in more funds for student activities and services. The president responded that additional classes would be staffed with part-time faculty members but that the remainder of the money would find a happy home in the district building fund.

Several administrators believed the district would continue to serve more students with less money until something broke. "We're at the straining point now. We are admitting deaf students, and they require an enormous amount of assistance, and it's very expensive." Supplies and equipment seemed to be less of a problem than space and staff, although even here a number of problems emerged. A library staff member said that the book budget had remained at $15,000 for six years and that the larger part of that amount had to be used to replace books stolen or damaged. English faculty members talked about the problems of obtaining paper, interspersing their comments with caustic remarks about recruiting brochures mailed every other week.

This situation caused Oakwood administrators to exercise the utmost ingenuity in complying with district mandates while maintaining the existing operation without additional resources. In one example, the district conducted workshops and mandated the development of a "marketing approach" at each college to expand services and to identify potential new clients. Oakwood administrators prepared their plan for compliance and included a request for the necessary funding in their proposed budget. When funding for the plan was eliminated, a decision was made to rename an existing committee the "Task Force on

Marketing" called for by the district mandate. In this way, the college was able to give an appearance of compliance while continuing to devote available resources to maintaining its operation.

Because an important consideration was offering courses that produced rather than used revenue, even classes established for developmental students with the most serious reading deficiencies were expected to enroll twenty-five students. Some were overenrolled in order to improve the chances that all could pay their own way. The emphasis on increasing revenues also affected the development of technical programs. Many new programs observed at Oakwood and on other campuses of the district were, in reality, hybrids formed by novel recombinations of existing courses. Because of the constant concern about fiscal restraints, even when addressing the highest district priorities, many instructors and some administrators at Oakwood perceived the district's top priority as remaining solvent.

District Priorities and Faculty Commitment

We have noted that most full-time faculty members in the Richfield District were tenured and were represented by a strong faculty association. Concurrently, fiscal constraints made it difficult to achieve change by hiring new faculty members. Under such circumstances, how effective were key administrators in persuading existing faculty members to share their vision of the future?

A survey was used to evaluate faculty "commitment." We regarded faculty members as committed to a district priority to the extent that they (1) expressed loyalty to the priority, (2) agreed with its importance, and (3) actively supported its achievement (Salancik, 1977).

Most community colleges lack the traditions of collegiality and faculty autonomy found in universities, but the Richfield District was unique in having a tradition of strong faculty influence. While still a faculty member, the president of Oakwood had led a drive for greater faculty autonomy in the educational process. From his perspective, the battle to prevent administrative interference in the classroom had largely been won. One consequence was to create a set of circumstances in which faculty members could effectively resist change. Given the priorities established and the methods through which they were identified and supported, at both the district and the campus levels, how committed were Oakwood faculty members to district priorities? Equally important, what were the consequences for classroom literacy?

Not surprisingly, perceptions about the priority given to the developmental student at Oakwood were mixed. The dean of instruction, who had been instrumental in encouraging faculty members to improve services for developmental students, saw priorities shifting to accord developmental students greater emphasis. For a large number of instructors and administrators, however, such students appeared to have low priority. Instructors committed to the developmental programs at Oakwood perceived college administrative support for their efforts to be less consistent than they thought desirable. In addition, Oakwood staff members felt that the majority of administrators at the district level, with the exception of one vice-chancellor, neither understood the needs of underprepared students nor accorded a particularly high priority to meeting them.

Overall, the Oakwood faculty was more committed to developmental education than faculties on other campuses, partly because Oakwood had assumed a leadership role in this area within the district. Interestingly, however, a higher percentage of the faculty at Oakwood actively opposed developmental education, suggesting that progress in achieving a priority will mobilize the opposition, as well as the support.

Oakwood was not the most enthusiastic campus about serving the new clientele, as judged by the priority it gave to that endeavor. Again, the lack of enthusiasm seemed to be related to Oakwood's experience as a campus that was receiving more than its perceived share of nontraditional students. This observation was underscored by a comment from an Oakwood administrator in a meeting of the administrative council discussing the greater-than-expected success of the new basic skills program: "We're becoming a dumping ground for the district." Then he quickly corrected himself, "I mean a magnet school."

Among faculty members and department chairs, the strongest expressions of commitment were reserved for student retention and occupational education. In contrast, Oakwood administrators were most strongly committed to serving the new clientele, a difference in preferences we discuss further when examining the impact of administrative and faculty values. Significantly, department chairs at Oakwood showed the lowest levels of commitment to all four priorities of any college in the district. They were less committed than either Oakwood faculty members or other Oakwood administrators to the priorities of serving the new clientele and developmental education.

Hirschman's (1970) concepts of exit, voice, and loyalty were useful in describing the faculty at Oakwood. Because of the current job market for instructors, the exit option was acted out through withdrawal from all activities except those related directly to the classroom or required by written faculty policies. The concept of "exit" seemed more accurate than the more popular term *burned out,* often used by faculty members in referring to themselves. Those exercising the exit option frequently remained committed to their colleagues, to the students whom they believed belonged at Oakwood, and to their teaching. They were simply unreachable so far as institutional priorities were concerned. Because they were unreachable regardless of the strategies administrators used, there was no way of altering their behavior as a result of administrative initiative.

Faculty members whom we classified as loyal to institutional priorities tended to be those more recently employed, partly because candidates for new faculty positions were carefully screened for both the competencies and the attitudes required to contribute to institutional priorities. Because of a relatively recent emphasis on affirmative action, new faculty groups also contained a disproportionate percentage of women and minorities. Over time, there was a tendency for loyal faculty members to move toward the exit option as they encountered limited resources, passive resistance or indifference from a majority of their colleagues, and active resistance from the third segment of the faculty, the "voice group."

Faculty members exercising the voice option resisted actively and verbally the achievement of institutional priorities through their departments and the faculty association. This group received a high percentage of total administrative attention, despite its limited numbers, because it was so visible. Administrators acted to combat the criticism when it surfaced, to prevent it from surfacing when possible, and to move critics to positions where they could do the least harm. Many faculty members in the voice category were committed to the institution despite the discrepancies between their values and those of key administrators. As a kind of "loyal opposition," they contributed by keeping administrators aware of the limits of acceptable change without incurring unacceptable costs.

The number of loyal faculty members or administrators varied both with the priority and with the amount of progress being made in achieving it. Categorizing faculty members or administrators other than with regard to specific priorities was therefore a risky proposition. The same faculty member or administrator exercising voice in the area of developmental education might be in the exit category, or even demonstrating loyalty, in less controversial areas such as student retention or occupational education. The exit, or uncommitted, category included a significant number of Oakwood and of district faculty members for all priorities. Clearly, the problem of achieving commitment to institutional priorities was a serious problem for a change-minded administration.

A large number of Oakwood instructors remained uncommitted to all district priorities throughout the study. For each of the priorities, however, there were sufficient committed instructors to permit progress, provided that the level of resistance could be controlled. Staff development activities and planning were instrumental in keeping resistance to manageable levels, as previously noted.

Perhaps the most important contribution of both the planning process and staff development activities was to redefine normative expectations. Because administrators controlled the process of disseminating information and gave significant publicity to the outcomes of planning activities and staff development sessions, there was little doubt in anyone's mind about what the priorities actually were. Instructors therefore had only a few options. They could choose to commit themselves to the achievement of administratively defined priorities and, by so doing, qualify for the rewards made available in the form of released time, supplementary pay, and, perhaps, an administrative appointment. Alternatively, they could choose to resist institutional priorities, thereby incurring the threat of sanctions. In the Richfield District, given the high job security of instructors, the threat of sanctions was not a significant deterrent. Finally, instructors could opt for covert resistance or simply transfer their energies to activities outside the institution, such as businesses or avocational interests.

Impact of Values on Commitment. Administrators and faculty members in the Richfield District brought different values to the change process. Administrators were growth-oriented. For them, a major indicator of success was an increase in the numbers of full-time student equivalents. Growth also resulted in budget increases, bringing the flexibility to initiate new services. Faculty members, by contrast, were concerned about the impact of additional growth on already-crowded facilities, as well as the effect of an increasingly diverse student clientele on their ability to teach and to experience success as they defined it.

The majority of the full-time faculty were described by administrators as not supporting the open-access philosophy. This faculty position was attributed to the history of the college and to the fact that Oakwood had been a predominantly transfer institution. Interviews with faculty members, however, suggested that their objections to the open-access philosophy centered on two concerns: the availability of resources and the probability of success for the more limited students. They felt that the quality of instruction and the reputation of the college had been damaged by the stress on increasing full-time student equivalents and the recruitment of poorly prepared students. They disagreed with the practice of providing credit toward an associate degree for courses designed to help students improve reading, writing, and mathematics skills at very basic levels. They were concerned about the impact on transfer and occupational programs of diverting scarce resources to serve the new clientele.

Administrators prized innovation and problem solving as appropriate responses to what they perceived as a need to change the educational program and services to make them more responsive to the external community. Faculty members resisted administratively directed innovation and belittled the use of outside experts brought in to tell them how to improve. Administrators were concerned with numbers; faculty members were concerned with process. Administrators believed that every adult not being served by some other type of institution was an appropriate focus for community college recruiting activity. Faculty members preferred to restrict their efforts to students who exhibited the characteristics they regarded as essential for success in the college parallel or career programs.

Instructors perceived district goals as "keeping the machinery operating" by offering anything that sold and by retaining a higher percentage of those who enrolled. They saw their own primary commitment as focusing on the traditional student. Their position was not an absolute refusal to consider services for the new student clientele. Rather, it represented concern about the availability of resources and the possibility that using resources to address the needs of nontraditional students would diminish the quality of the transfer and occupational programs. The difference of opinion between administration and faculty became particularly intense when instructors unsympathetic to the concept of developmental education were asked to relinquish transfer courses to visiting staff members so that they could teach remedial students.

Aside from the philosophical issue of whether low-ability students should be admitted at all, there was no agreement on what should happen to students as a result of their enrollment in programs designed for the underprepared. Even instructors teaching in the same department disagreed about what developmental programs ought to achieve and whether the students enrolled in such programs should even be served by the college.

Instructors who worked directly with non-English-speaking and underprepared students appeared compassionate and concerned about them. In contrast, instructors who had little or no contact with these students were critical of their presence at Oakwood. The attitudes and comments of the majority of the faculty who did not work with seriously underprepared students increased the pressures on those who did and contributed to the impression that the latter were engaged in teaching subject matter and students whose presence in a community college was somehow highly suspect.

Faculty members' concerns about the desirability and feasibility of serving remedial students were aggravated by their perceptions of district objectives as growth for the sake of becoming larger. They believed that enrollment growth was always the first concern of administrators, as evidenced through such statements as "Bodies are money. The district can translate these into full-time equivalencies, and the state pays for them." The district emphasis on enrolling underprepared students was seen as a response to the alternative of a declining enrollment. The priority placed on reducing attrition was attributed to similar motives. Instructors believed that the causes of attrition were largely out of their hands, being related to such factors as transportation, family problems, and jobs. Many perceived the emphasis on retention as an alternative administrative strategy to the recruitment of more students and as an extension of the concern with bodies rather than with education. These instructors found the college slogan used in advertising. "Oakwood is the right place to be," offensive and misleading. They felt that the slogan promised the college would be all things to all people.

Programmatic Consequences. The problems of responding to district priorities, given the absence of commitment from chairs and other faculty members, was apparent in department responses to the district priority of providing more opportunities in developmental education. In departments that could not escape responding, such as English, reading, and mathematics, much of the work of developing and teaching new courses was accomplished by new faculty members employed specifically for that purpose. In mathematics, the department never formally approved a new course offered, nominally under its auspices, by a relatively new faculty member. Several departments had never considered the need for developmental courses in their area of responsibility and indicated they had no intention of doing so. Two major departments, social science and business, appointed committees to study the need for developmental education. These committees met for a year and disbanded without having reached any agreement on recommendations to be advanced.

Sections of the below-100-level remedial courses were limited by department scheduling decisions. A participant observer working at the basic studies table at registration reported that all below-100-level English courses closed out early in registration. Although placement testing continued and many students were referred to these courses, no further sections were added.

At first it seemed strange that faculty members should be resistant to a priority designed to place "new" students in appropriate courses and thus keep them out of the courses they did not have the reading and writing skills to handle. However, for some faculty members, resistance to district priorities and district encroachment on campus operations was a way of life. For others, resistance was targeted directly at the intent of the program. Previous remedial courses, at least, had attempted to mainstream students; theoretically, students who made it through those courses were prepared to enter the regular college curriculum. The new basic skills program had as its purpose, however, "assisting individuals to obtain the necessary skills to function in society." Such a statement appeared to legitimize teaching basic skills for the sake of teaching basic skills. Further, it encouraged attendance by students who would never enter a degree-oriented curriculum. This was clearly contrary to the purposes for which many faculty members believed the college existed.

A minority of faculty members were able to achieve change in the absence of active opposition from their colleagues, as demonstrated by the establishment of the basic skills program. Of course, the dean had previously ensured the existence of the cadre of necessary full-time faculty members to design and implement the program through judicious recruitment for the few faculty vacancies authorized during the preceding two years.

Where astute and meticulous planning was absent, efforts to adapt programs could easily fail because of the extensive constraints operating. In the same year that Oakwood started its basic skills program with full enrollment, a similar effort in a sister college serving a student population with at least as many educational deficiencies failed to enroll any students. The sister college also received discretionary district funds for the proposed program but did not benefit from the careful planning that produced success at Oakwood.

Not all efforts to change programs and services at Oakwood to respond to district priorities proceeded as smoothly as the development of the basic skills program. Just as the "rules for change" at Oakwood made it possible for small groups of committed faculty members to achieve change in the absence of active opposition, the presence of opposition made it possible for small groups to block change or significantly alter its direction. When the need for faculty assistance with a new process for advising and registering students was discussed at a meeting of the administrative council, a faculty representative in attendance stated, "The faculty had better be consulted, or they will blow their tops." Eventually, as discussed in Chapter Seven, it proved necessary to involve all faculty members in the advising process, even though administration preferred to include only those regarded as able to do an effective job, because the faculty refused to support a process that involved more time for some than for others.

Summary Discussion

To what extent were new priorities supported at Oakwood, and what impact did they have on classrooms and on classroom literacy? Clearly, the priority of attracting a new clientele was being achieved at a level and with results that were distressing to some instructors and administrators. The developmental program had been expanded and changed. Perhaps it had been improved, but the evidence for such a conclusion was lacking. Students who were underprepared were kept from regular courses. New courses with greater emphasis on basic reading and writing skills had been developed and staffed. An altered registration and advising system for a time channeled students with the requisite qualifications into these courses.

On the less positive side, developmental instructors received less support from administrators than they perceived as necessary, raising questions about the level of administrative commitment to this priority at both district and college levels.

The situation was less clear in the area of retention. Students in developmental offerings did persist. At the same time, there were significant issues related to the progress of those who persisted and their motivations for remaining at Oakwood. Many administrators and instructors alike saw the primary motivation as a desire to remain eligible for student assistance as an alternative to welfare. Further, there was no evidence that persistence in transfer or occupational programs was influenced by the priority placed on retention. Perhaps, as instructors believed, many of the causes of attrition were beyond their control.

Occupational education emerged as an operative goal at the district level rather late in the study. The problems were clearly identified. Space for new career programs was limited, and much equipment for existing programs was outdated. Developing new programs under these conditions through use of adjunct staff was attempted but with limited results. After a year of extensive effort, a five-year plan was developed and was approved by the governing board. With approval came a first-year funding commitment of $5 million.

This analysis of district priorities and the adaptive responses of Oakwood raises the issue of the relation between change and conflict. Those priorities toward which Oakwood made the greatest progress served as lightning rods attracting not only the normal resistance to new approaches but, in addition, the reservoir of ill will generated by previous district actions in trying to implement change. Some instructors might not have resisted serving the new clientele and developmental education had it not been for the establishment of the college without walls and the expanded role for adjuncts. A good case can be made, however, for the proposition that without significant change Richfield would never have closed the gap between key administrators' concerns for a new, underserved clientele and the historical emphasis on serving traditional students, primarily through the transfer curriculum.

Attempts to change educational programs and services must concurrently produce commitment among instructors and administrators involved in achieving the change while lessening commitment to previous and competing objectives among the majority of instructors and administrators from whom nothing more than acquiescence is required. The administrative strategies most evident at Oakwood in relation to this process were selecting new staff, participation in planning, and formal staff development programs. The results attainable through the strategies available were limited mainly because there were few opportunities for employing new staff, perhaps the most effective approach to developing new programs or services.

No standards exist for determining when levels of commitment become sufficiently low among instructors or administrators to endanger achievement of organizational priorities. At Oakwood, more progress had been made with faculty members than with administrators in the critical area of developmental education, as evidenced by the comparative percentages of the two groups exercising the voice option in this area. The fact that one fourth of instructors were committed to serving the new clientele and one third to developmental education indicated substantial support for these priorities, particularly in view of the relatively small number of instructors likely to provide active opposition.

However, the absence of faculty leadership (other than from quasi-administrators) in identifying desired change may be a severe limitation in efforts to make educational programs and services more responsive to new clients. Department chairs, who might have provided leadership, reported lower levels of commitment to all priorities than any other group. In effect, leadership for change came from a deeply divided administrative staff and from quasi-administrators, whose lack of administrative authority made them easy targets for faculty opposition.

Our discussion of commitment appears to assume that the major task facing administrators is to devise ways of increasing faculty commitment to the goals that the administrators perceive as having central importance. But suppose administrative priorities have unintended and largely unrecognized consequences for a major societal concern such as literacy, as we have suggested in our chapters on classroom activities. If what we observed at Oakwood is generally true among open-door colleges, and we believe it is, then the emphasis on access and serving new clients, when implemented in the absence of effective advisement, defined levels of achievement for students entering programs, and established standards for assessing progress, contributes directly to the decline in critical literacy.

In the concluding chapter, we consider the implications of this study for instructors and administrators in open-door colleges. Finally, we offer recommendations for reversing the current trends for those who believe, as we do, that the failure to emphasize critical literacy may create technically competent citizens whose inability to use written and oral language effectively will bar the upward mobility they might otherwise experience.

CHAPTER NINE

❧ ❧ ❧

Promoting Critical Literacy in College

❧ ❧ ❧

During the past two decades, important changes have occurred in the way we define the outcomes of a college education. Many of these changes center on the literacy we expect of the college educated in contrast to the general population. An advancing technology has altered the priorities we attach to reading or composing written language, and the consequences for critical literacy have by no means been confined to open-access colleges. But allowing for technology and the changes that have affected all institutions, there still seem to be grounds for special concern about the extent to which open-access colleges have contributed to a process of leveling down, rather than leveling up, through a deemphasis of critical literacy.

Students we observed at Oakwood needed assistance in making use of written information, engaged in little analysis or evaluation of the information they received, and did not relate their literacy activities to clear educational goals. This lack of active and engaged language use provided little opportunity for students to acquire skill in self-directed inquiry or the flexibility necessary to adapt effectively to a rapidly changing social and work environment.

Individuals disturbed by these conclusions may argue that our study site was atypical and our findings in error. However, recent surveys, as discussed in Chapter Three, also suggest the limited reading and writing expectations at many community colleges. In addition, the National Institute of Education, which funded our study, concurrently funded a study of literacy conducted by the University of Texas at Austin in two urban community colleges. The two studies, carried out independently but concurrently, have reached strikingly similar conclusions, as the following passages from the report of the Texas study indicate:

> There are, however, grave concerns which arise from our findings that students come to expect, through their college experiences, that reading and writing are not important in themselves— that instructors do not demand anything from them beyond brief, disjointed passages of reading for specific information or writing of disjointed responses to specific, narrow questions.
>
> The reduction of reading and writing tasks to those performative activities that extract information from context that require no demonstration of synthesis/comprehension of larger issues cannot be construed as ever improving or developing students' abilities to read and write [Roueche and Comstock, 1981, pp. 1-45, 1-61].

This similarity in findings is the first of several discussed in this chapter. Although we did not intend to produce a definitive statement about the status of literacy in all community colleges, we do propose hypotheses on how current practices are likely to affect the quality of students' learning experiences.

Community colleges have had a central role in providing opportunities for upward mobility. If their students are to compete effectively for professional, managerial, and technical jobs, however, they will have to require independent, critical, and expressive uses of language. In other words, to preserve the "opportunity function," particularly for minorities who have gravitated to open-access community colleges in disproportionate numbers, community colleges must attend to critical literacy development.

In the two years between the completion of our study and the preparation of this book, Oakwood has joined a growing number of colleges that are seeking ways to deal with the issues we have raised. In this concluding chapter, we identify some of the alternatives available to institutions as they formulate explicit literacy policies. We begin by reviewing the complex set of interrelated factors that contributed to the decreased emphasis on critical literacy at Oakwood and then suggest administrative strategies that can begin to reverse this decline.

Institutional Characteristics and Policies

The institutional characteristics that Oakwood College displayed during the time of our study are illustrated in Figure 5. They evolved from responses to key issues addressing who the college should serve, what should be done for those served, and who should pay for the services provided. The position that Oakwood and the Richfield District took in relation to these three issues resulted increasingly in expanded educational mission, diversity of clientele, and emphasis on sheer numbers of enrollments.

Expanded Mission. Since the Richfield District answered the question of whom the community college should serve by saying "everyone" or "the total community" and did not establish priorities on what should be done for those who attended, all educational activities were given equal merit. During the period of our study, Richfield expanded its educational activities and, of necessity, broadened the requirements of what was acceptable literacy. Because standards for the new activities were not identified, demands for critical literacy declined to a sort of "least common denominator."

Richfield's response to the question of who should pay for new educational services was to continue its efforts to increase state support. Since Richfield, like most community college districts, did not receive funding from the state for its non-credit offerings (Breneman and Nelson, 1981), the district faced

Figure 5. Impact of Institutional Priorities on College Literacy.

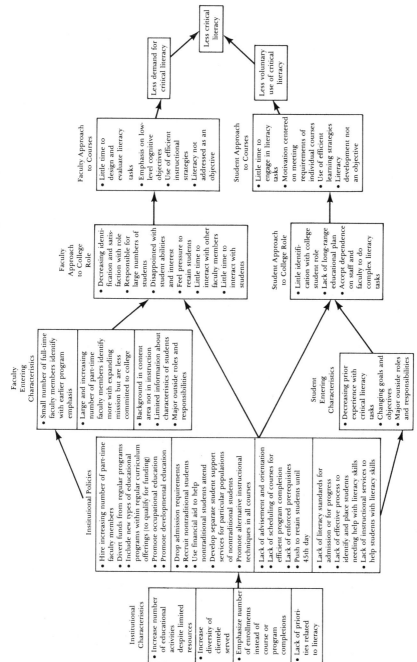

an almost irresistible temptation to offer as many courses for credit as possible. Doing so meant that courses unintended for transfer were mixed with those traditionally a part of the transfer offerings. Further, the special funding allocated for "occupational courses" resulted in this designation being overused.

Increasing the number of remedial courses also required fancy footwork. The Richfield District was reimbursed for students enrolled in remedial courses the same as for students in transfer courses. But with the necessity of keeping enrollments in remedial classes small, larger numbers had to be enrolled in transfer and occupational courses to offset the losses in revenue that resulted from smaller classes. Increases in class size had an impact on literacy; instructors often cited class size as a major factor in deciding to avoid writing assignments and to use multiple choice instead of essay examinations.

Most students requiring developmental studies courses also needed financial aid. To remain eligible for financial aid, they were required by federal regulations to complete twelve hours of credit work applicable to a degree each semester. This placed Oakwood in the administratively and ethically precarious position of awarding credit toward an associate degree for work that essentially paralleled some of the more basic competencies taught in elementary schools. Before each registration, faculty members had to find enough credit courses where students' lack of reading and writing skills would not handicap instructors or other students.

The strategies adopted by the Richfield District to promote an expanded mission created opposition from faculty. The most visible strategy, the creation of a new college-without-walls, became the focus for much vocal criticism. Responsibilities for many of the off-campus credit and noncredit courses previously provided by the campus colleges were transferred to the new institution. In addition, its educational activities were defined to include alternative modes of instruction (radio and television, for example), as well as training at industrial sites and supervision of a preexisting skills center offering entry-level occupational training.

The new college-without-walls became a center for innovation within the district, achieving many of the goals it had been established to pursue. At the same time, it competed with the campus-based colleges for increasingly scarce resources, hired an exclusively part-time faculty, and pursued priorities that conflicted with the preferences of most faculty members and a number of influential legislators. Throughout the study, the decision to establish the college-without-walls remained a volatile and controversial issue.

Such strategies as establishing a college-without-walls were both a response to an increasingly diverse clientele and a contribution to even greater diversity among those enrolling in the Richfield District. In effect, it was a chicken-and-egg situation. But as new educational activities evolved either to serve new clientele or to attract them, the issue of quality in relation to available resources became increasingly important.

Diversity of Clientele. The Richfield District sought to expand enrollments, at least partly to increase its resource base. Beyond accepting all who came, Richfield used aggressive marketing techniques and extensive advertising to reach new segments of the population not previously served. Because these techniques were used during a period when the numbers of students in the traditional eighteen- to twenty-four-year-old range had peaked, the inevitable result was the attraction of a more diverse clientele—both in objectives and in previous academic preparation. Those interested in pursuing credit courses and degree programs came to constitute a smaller percentage of those attending, and more students required remediation.

To help serve more nontraditional students, Oakwood encouraged alternative methods of instruction in all classrooms. By implication, the best instructors were those who used audio-visual materials, provided study guides, and efficiently transmitted the content necessary for meeting class requirements. These strategies, as previously noted, made it less necessary for students to independently learn or compose connected language. The few students at Oakwood who by preference engaged in such learning and composing activities experienced criticism from instructors and their fellow students, a phenomenon also reported by London (1978) and Neumann and Riesman (1980).

Special services were created to meet the in-class and out-of-class needs of students who lacked the academic preparation, language skills, or support systems to survive on their own. Initially, such services were funded out of special grants and were developed, in part, so that other instructors and support staff would be minimally affected. Very soon, however, it became evident that college-wide changes were necessary if the institution was to adequately serve the diverse students recruited to maintain or increase enrollments.

Emphasis on FTSE. FTSE was indeed the name of the game in the Richfield District. After each registration, Oakwood administrators were elated or subdued, depending on their enrollment and rate of growth in relation to other district colleges. Their interest in enrollment rather than program, or even course, completion was understandable given Richfield's enrollment-driven funding formula and the predominance of students without clear educational goals. At the same time, Oakwood's "efficient" strategies for enrolling students in courses may have contributed to low completion rates by discouraging or, at best, by failing to assist those who were interested in degree programs.

The substantial increase in part-time faculty members who were not expected to advise students left the burden of providing all advising to the relatively constant number of full-time faculty members. In turn, to avoid unacceptable increases in faculty work loads, full-time faculty members were forced by necessity to seek efficient strategies for getting students into classes.

Because low completion rates were taken for granted, there was little pressure to schedule courses to optimize students' opportunities to complete a sequence within two years. The argument that a particular advanced course needed to be offered, despite low enrollments, because some students required it for graduation, was not persuasive. In addition, to ensure sufficient enrollment many advanced courses did not carry prerequisites.

Roueche and Comstock (1981) pointed to lack of coherence in instructional programs, as well as lack of effective advising, as major problems in the Texas community colleges they studied. On these campuses and at Oakwood, the institutional emphasis on enrollment had an impact on literacy—one that was most evident in the way students and instructors viewed their respective roles in the classroom. For students without explicit educational goals, meeting requirements was the way to deal with a series of essentially discrete courses. The absence of advising left students who had very limited understanding of what constituted a college education free to negotiate their own paths through the curriculum. Faculty members were not happy with this situation, but they felt powerless to intervene. One consequence was that they became increasingly detached from the institution and its priorities. Instructors' acceptance of their inability to reverse prevailing trends was one more factor contributing to the reduced emphasis on critical literacy.

Lack of a Literacy Policy. Perhaps as a consequence of the priority placed on mission expansion and enrollment growth, Oakwood had no explicit policies on literacy. Specifically, it had not formulated literacy standards for admission or degree completion, instituted substantial procedures to identify and place students needing help with literacy skills, or developed strategies for promoting critical literacy. Although the number of basic skills courses had increased, there was little articulation between these courses and the reading and writing behaviors expected in existing courses.

The Texas colleges studied by Roueche and Comstock (1981) also lacked a policy on literacy development. They noted the absence of effective procedures to identify and place students who needed help with literacy skills, yet poor placement was only one aspect of the problem. In both Oakwood and the Texas colleges, existing language skills courses did not deal with skills used in other courses, and instructors in content courses did not offer literacy instruction. Instructors felt free to drop literacy requirements, since they saw that most students lacked the skills to fulfill them. Moreover, instructors contributed to the students' view that written language was simply a means of meeting course requirements. Overall, there was little reason to expect students in any course to be concerned about developing critical literacy skills.

Because even modal students lacked critical literacy skills, something more than a peripheral basic skills or developmental program was required—namely, a college-wide effort. Literacy development should have been an educational objective in all facets of the curriculum. Faculty members should have been designing strategies to help students develop literacy skills while administrators should have been designing a delivery system to accommodate the majority of students.

The lack of a literacy policy in an institution that was expanding its enrollments and educational activities created an environment where there was little incentive for students to use more complex forms of language. This environment had a pervasive influence on instructors and students and on the teaching and learning strategies they adopted in the classroom.

Faculty and Student Issues

Faculty. Oakwood faculty members seemed increasingly less satisfied with their role and less committed to the college and its priorities. Many had major responsibilities outside the college that absorbed their time and interest. Full-time faculty members were tenured, highly paid, and secure in their positions. Hired during the sixties, they identified with the transfer emphasis of that period and had little commitment to the goal of serving a new clientele. Part-time faculty members, though more open to changing conceptions of the college mission, had little commitment to institutional priorities because of their marginal status. Neither full-time nor part-time instructors interacted to any significant degree with other faculty members or with students; faculty meetings were minimal, informal networks weak and office hours brief. Aside from teaching individual courses, most faculty members had shallow connections with the college.

The hiring practices of the district meant that faculty members had a strong background in their content areas through previous training or, in the case of occupational instructors, work experience. They generally were not well-grounded in curriculum and instruction or in the characteristics of the student population they taught.

Given their backgrounds and the institutional priorities

of Oakwood, faculty members approached the role of instructor with an eye to efficiency and minimal involvement. Large course loads and class sizes, combined with extensive outside responsibilities and frequent overloads, left little time for instructional design and evaluation. Because research papers and essay exams are time-consuming for instructors as well as students, such methods of evaluation tended to disappear in the face of other activities. Instructors were likely to eliminate these tasks because they perceived students' work as inferior and, therefore, even more time-consuming to evaluate. In addition, instructors experienced institutional pressure to adopt alternative teaching strategies for their diverse clientele. Confronted with these various demands, instructors chose to preserve content at the expense of requirements for critical literacy. Untrained in instructional methods, they made no attempt to integrate the teaching of basic skills and content.

The Texas report presented a similar analysis of instructional strategies. Roueche and Comstock (1981, pp. xiii, xiv) summarized the impact of these strategies on classroom literacy: "Reading and writing are not required across the curriculum in purposeful ways. Instructional and evaluative strategies typically involve low-level cognitive activities. . . . Diverse student populations bring a wide range of abilities to classrooms. Instructors who attempt to provide instruction for all may feel compelled to make literacy demands at the lowest cognitive levels to accommodate the greatest numbers."

Students. Like faculty members, students experienced competing demands on their time. Modal Oakwood students attended part-time, worked, and had major family responsibilities. They came to the campus to attend particular courses. Interaction with other students and with instructors outside courses was minimal. Limited advisement or orientation beyond that required to enroll in individual courses provided little incentive for developing long-range educational plans. Under such circumstances, it was not surprising that students preferred to learn discrete "bits" of information, relying on faculty and staff members to simplify or accomplish for them the more complex literacy tasks.

At Oakwood, as in the Texas study, students took the

path of least resistance by finding out what the instructor wanted and providing it. They would identify important content (material written on the board or in teacher-prepared handouts) and restrict themselves to that content when they discovered it was all they were required to know. In this way, students' strategies matched their instructors'. Having limited time and competing demands, they met requirements through efficient learning strategies, emphasizing the use of fragmented language.

Of course, there were exceptions to the modal "requirement meeters." In both the Oakwood and Texas studies, some students identified strongly with the student role and enjoyed learning for its own sake. Others planned specific applications of the information they learned. Both these groups engaged in more critical forms of literacy. Most students, however, had only a vague idea of how any single course related to goals and were motivated primarily by grades and credit attainment.

The Oakwood and Texas colleges, with their requirement meeters, part-time faculty, and external pressures to increase enrollment, did little to encourage critical literacy development. A series of policy changes will be required to change this situation.

Reversing the Trend

Some of the forces that have reduced the emphasis on critical literacy seem rooted in the broader social context and hence are beyond the reach of those who lead community colleges. From this perspective, it is tempting to view Oakwood and similar community colleges as making the best of unfortunate circumstances over which they have little or no control. On closer examination, however, it is clear that community colleges not only are influenced by their social context but seek to influence it, often with unintended results.

Much has been written about the effects of enrollment-driven funding formulas on community colleges. Such formulas are established by state legislators who have been relatively uninfluenced by extensive information about the adverse effect of such formulas on the mission that community colleges have carved out. In a number of states legislators have systematically reduced the level of support by refusing to increase the maximum contribution as costs have risen, thus throwing more of the burden on local communities or user fees. As Breneman and Nelson (1981, p. 161) put it, "Consensus about the scope, purpose, and value of numerous two-year college activities is more to be found in the rhetoric than in the reality."

College administrators have too often chosen to pursue mission expansion in the absence of consensus and adequate resources. This expansion has been funded by such stopgap techniques as employing more part-time instructors and increasing average class sizes. The administrative decision to use marketing techniques to increase the number and diversity of clients was based on two assumptions—first, that numbers would prove persuasive in resolving debates over mission and funding and, second, that legislators would continue to honor funding formulas no matter how rapid the growth in enrollments. Both assumptions have proved false. As a consequence, larger numbers of students with more serious academic deficiencies have been served from a dwindling resource base, and existing programs and services have borne the burden of making up the difference.

These policy decisions, which have altered the forms of literacy emphasized in community colleges, are by no means irreversible. However, community colleges have moved away from an emphasis on critical literacy over a period of more than twenty years. It is unrealistic to expect any dramatic reversals to occur quickly. Nevertheless, there are enough signs on the horizon in such places as Miami-Dade, Essex County (New Jersey), and the College of DuPage in Illinois, as well as at Oakwood and its sister colleges, to suggest that the prognosis may now be much more optimistic than any of us would have guessed during the study.

The policy changes necessary for promoting more critical literacy behaviors among community college students are summarized in Table 2. We have presented the polar extremes for each policy area. The policies of most institutions would be somewhere between the two extremes. During the 1960s and

Table 2. Promoting Critical Literacy: Policy Alternatives.

Policy Area	"Bitting" Less Use of Critical Literacy	"Texting" More Use of Critical Literacy
Admission and Placement	Recruit actively. Seek new clientele. Admit all who apply, with enrollment permitted in any course for which there is no quota (for example, nursing).	Recruit selectively. Admit all who apply with high school equivalency, with enrollment limited to courses that match student reading, writing, and math skills.
Financial Assistance	Keep all students eligible for as much assistance as possible for as long as possible through credit for basic skills, liberal interpretation of regulations, and easy withdrawal policies.	Limit eligibility to students making defined progress toward a degree or certificate according to some acceptable time frame.
Educational Program	Design program to offer "all things to all people." Seek to emphasize community rather than college. Avoid setting priorities.	Limit to programs and courses that can be offered at a defined level of quality within the limits of existing or probable resources. Emphasize degree-oriented occupational or transfer programs.
Course Designations	Label courses to maximize funding potential. Place burden on transfer institutions and state agencies to disprove course status.	Label courses according to the objectives and academic experience of those for whom they are designed.
Program for Remediation	Emphasize courses and services described as developmental and administered by a separate unit. Include goals such as socialization having equal status with the remediation of academic deficiencies.	Emphasize remedial courses in academic skill areas administered by related departments. May include support services such as tutoring and study skills courses.
Promotion of Academic Progress	Facilitate continuing enrollment by liberal withdrawal regulations and nonpunitive grading. Define achievement as grade-point average for courses completed and surveys of student satisfaction, as well as reports on selected individuals.	Require students to qualify for regular status in a degree or certificate program within some limited and specific period of time. Require defined progress toward achieving educational objectives. Define achievements as completion of defined sequence with minimum grade-point average in required courses. Use standardized or teacher developed examinations of academic achievement.
Faculty Conditions	Use part-time instructors extensively as a strategy for expanding services despite resource constraints. The ratio of full-time faculty to students justifies neglect of advisement and orientation procedures.	Limit use of part-time instructors to the coverage of enrollment fluctuations or where necessary skills cannot be obtained in a full-time faculty member. Full-time instructors expected to provide sound student advisement.

1970s, community colleges moved toward the left end of the continuum by adopting policies designed to expand mission and clientele by focusing on enrollments rather than completions. The more serious effects of these decisions on literacy were not evident until shrinking resources forced an enormous expansion in the use of part-time instructors, accompanied by gradual disintegration of the curriculum as a coherent program of study. In the following pages we discuss interrelated strategies for achieving what we believe to be a better balance between serving everyone to some minimum degree and preserving the traditional emphasis on opportunity for upward social and economic mobility.

Admissions and Placement. Central to any strategy for promoting emphasis on texting and critical literacy is the admissions process. To the extent that the admissions process functions primarily as an efficient operation for getting as many people as possible into saleable course offerings, there is limited opportunity for establishing classroom environments that encourage critical literacy. We propose, therefore, a different view of admissions.

The concept of open admissions is pivotal to the purpose for which community colleges were established; altering this aspect of admissions would change community colleges in a way that would be unacceptable to many of their proponents. Nevertheless, it would be possible to require some minimum level of achievement as a prerequisite for enrollment in any credit course or degree program. High school graduation or attainment of a general equivalency degree would appear to be an appropriate minimum. Because every community provides opportunities for individuals to gain either of these credentials, no one would be arbitrarily excluded from admission to a community college. Persons who were unable or unwilling to satisfy the high school equivalency requirement would still be able to enroll in community service offerings, but credit-free courses should be clearly differentiated from degree-related work.

Beyond requiring minimal evidence of previous academic achievement, admission procedures should be aimed at matching student abilities and objectives with appropriate college programs. Entrance and exit competencies should be defined for each transfer and occupational program, including requirements for reading and writing.

In addition to measuring aptitude or achievement, open-access colleges may need to consider placing students according to their objectives, a recommendation that has already been advanced by at least one major commission (Astin, 1982). The importance of objectives as distinct from ability in determining student learning strategies and performance in coursework is one of the most significant findings of the Oakwood study.

There is nothing particularly new in the suggestion that community colleges should define and enforce entering and exit requirements. This practice has been followed for some time in the health-related fields, where program costs and number of applicants require selectivity in determining who enters. What is new is the proposal that community colleges accept the responsibility for working with all applicants to determine the relation between their needs and interests and the programs offered, rather than following the efficient strategies for placing students in classes that were so prevalent at Oakwood to maximize enrollments. If students are to become more than simply efficient requirement meeters in the classroom, they must be given assistance in determining the relation between their educational goals and the courses in which they enroll. Oakwood staff members did not see such assistance as an important part of their responsibility. In particular, it was inconceivable that a student would be told candidly, "There is nothing for you here. Try a trade school or your local high school."

A degree of duplicity, however much unintended, exists in the practice of admitting all students to courses that will lead nowhere for many of them while practicing highly selective admissions in the more sought-after programs, such as nursing and dental hygiene. We suggest that appropriate entering qualifications be established for all programs and that applicants who lack them be given some reasonable period within which to prepare for program qualification. This policy alternative would exclude no one who had, or was willing to earn, the designated prerequisites. Implementing this alternative would have implications for such additional policy areas as developmental education and requirements for progress.

Financial Assistance. The practice at Oakwood, as at many other open-access colleges, was to qualify as many applicants for financial aid as possible for as long as possible. The success of this approach was evident in the high percentage of students who remained eligible for federal financial assistance while completing course work designed to improve reading and writing skills to the fourth-grade or eighth-grade level. Students who could not read or write Spanish or English and who could not speak English could nevertheless qualify for financial aid and earn twelve credits the following semester toward an associate in general education degree.

The alternative to these practices would be to limit financial assistance to those it was designed to serve. This could be accomplished by requiring students to meet prerequisites for admission to a degree program within a specified time period. Focusing financial assistance on those making discernible progress toward an educational objective appropriate to college would remove much of the ambiguity that currently shrouds the purposes of student financial assistance in community colleges.

Tightening up on financial assistance policies would reduce enrollments in community colleges like Oakwood and would undoubtedly produce hardships for students with little hope of ever completing any degree or certificate program that Oakwood offered. However, it would free resources at Oakwood to improve the learning environment for critical literacy for those who remained.

Educational Programs. It seems clear that the decision to offer the basic skills program at Oakwood was a consequence of admitting students who lacked the proficiencies and motivations to benefit from what was already available. The decision to shape an educational program in response to the characteristics of those who show up, either because of open admissions or because of aggressive marketing techniques, is a manifestation of the "all things to all people" approach. This philosophy was understandable during an era when our nation lacked enough credentialed persons to take available jobs and policy makers were committed to the societal advantages of more education for everyone. But times change, and arguments for public subsidy *without regard to any visible results of such further education* are no longer persuasive.

Community colleges can respond to these changes in the external environment in a manner that emphasizes critical literacy if they establish priorities among program options, define expected outcomes, and set funding levels to ensure their achievement (Richardson and Leslie, 1980). For example, administrators could negotiate reductions in class size or teaching loads in return for the reintroduction of writing requirements emphasizing texting. Of course, such a change would have to be accompanied by corollary changes in admissions practices to ensure that students entering such classes were aware of and prepared for the new focus.

A decision to emphasize quality at the expense of quantity would mean establishing degree-oriented transfer and occupational programs as a funding priority and limiting the number of students served to a level for which adequate funding was available. Again, a probable consequence would be a reduction in total enrollments and the exercise of greater selectivity in determining who would be served. Given current fiscal constraints, however, the choice seems to be between serving everyone at such a minimal level that the credibility of all offerings is called into question or serving a more restricted clientele in programs with defined and observable outcomes.

In the best of all possible worlds, there would be no need to establish program priorities in an institution philosophically committed to serving all who seek admission. In the real world of the 1980s, administrators must make choices or run the risk of their institutions losing credibility in the functional areas where they receive greatest support and where they have the opportunity to make the most critical differences in the lives of those they serve.

Course Designations. From a dollars-and-cents perspective, it made sense for Oakwood to try to qualify as many courses as possible for reimbursement under the bonus formula used to fund career education courses. Revenues were further enhanced when as many as possible of the remainder were designated as transfer offerings. To be avoided were the credit-free designations for which no state reimbursement was provided.

Instructors contributed to the problem by proposing courses that universities offer in the junior and senior years. Since the majority of students take a few courses and never go on to a four-year institution, why not give them what they want and let the university take the heat for denying credit to the occasional student who subsequently does transfer?

From the perspectives of credibility and critical literacy, these arguments are much less persuasive. Blurring distinctions among courses has justified reducing literacy demands to a least common denominator. Universities question the integrity of courses that are offered without the usual prerequisites. One consequence is "upper-division creep," in which universities move more of their major courses into the upper division, creating difficulties for students who transfer as well as limiting the opportunity for community college instructors to teach preferred advanced classes in their disciplines. The cycle is complete when community colleges require substantial minimum enrollments in advanced courses, placing pressure on instructors to drop prerequisites as the price of being able to teach the course.

Part of the process for moving away from an emphasis on enrollments and toward an emphasis on outcomes involves establishing clear expectations for the level and type of literacy associated with courses designed to achieve programmatic objectives. Richfield took one major step in this direction when it standardized the outlines for transfer courses across the district. In addition to specifying content, however, appropriate literacy objectives should also be defined. Finally, the objectives and academic competencies of students enrolling in the course must be matched to the course's purpose, and instructors must be provided with the time and incentives to ensure that literacy goals as well as content requirements are addressed.

Program for Remediation. Twenty years ago a majority of the students who entered community colleges with academic deficiencies were left to sink or swim in regular college credit courses. Because most sank, remedial courses were developed to prepare students for the demands of the regular courses. As community colleges gained experience with remediation, it became apparent that the deficiencies accumulated over twelve or more years of elementary and secondary schooling were not to be corrected in a single semester; so additional sublevels of remedial courses were added. By the time we studied Oakwood, a student could take a full-time load for four semesters and never complete all the courses in the remedial sequence. As the number of courses increased, the goal was no longer preparation for regular coursework; it was taking students from "wherever they were to wherever they wanted to go" (Roueche and Snow, 1977). With success equated with persistence, the program at Oakwood measured up. Most students persisted even if they did not achieve the improvements in reading and writing originally established as objectives by the faculty. Almost none of these students succeeded according to the previous criterion of qualifying for admission to regular programs. Yet, all earned twelve credit hours each semester toward an associate in general education degree and remained eligible for financial assistance.

Despite administrative assurances that this program kept deficient students from taking up space in their classrooms, faculty members were critical of the program and of those who taught it. They did not believe the students belonged at Oakwood, and they resented some of the regulations on class size in their courses, which they saw as subsidizing the basic skills offerings. They were particularly hostile about the awarding of credit toward a degree because they believed the practice diminished the credibility of their other offerings.

There are, of course, alternatives available for coping with remediation so that a critical form of literacy is encouraged rather than inhibited. Since serving the academically deficient is a high-risk activity, attrition should be accepted as part of the cost of providing people with an opportunity. Utopian schemes for keeping all enrolled for as long as it takes them to achieve their objectives incorporate cost/benefit ratios that are quite unattractive to policy makers and the taxpaying public in the current environment. Under such circumstances, it seems reasonable to limit the scope of remediation to preparation for regular degree programs, require high school equivalency of all students, and set a maximum period of time during which students would be expected to complete a remedial sequence and qualify for admission. The Carnegie Commission on Higher Education (1970) recommended a foundation year, which seems appropriate, especially if adapted to the attendance patterns of part-time students. Remedial courses should be taught by the departments that offer advanced courses in the same fields. The math department should teach remedial math and the English department basic composition. Offering such courses under the auspices of a special developmental studies department practically ensures discontinuities between remedial and advanced courses in the same field. Learning laboratories and tutorial services should ensure that the cards are not stacked against the remedial student who is highly motivated and who can, with appropriate assistance, be ready for regular courses within a reasonable time period.

Community colleges, of course, are not prevented by any philosophical or academic reason from serving students who need more extensive instruction in basic skills. To be fair to these students and their instructors, the following conditions, as a minimum, should be observed: (1) Funding and policy bodies should acknowledge this mission explicitly in their written documents. (2) Special funding unrelated to the generation of academic credit hours should be provided. (3) Full-time faculty members with appropriate competencies and work schedules designed around the needs of teaching basic reading and writing should be employed. (4) Class size should recognize the need for individualization that accompanies dealing with most basic skills. (5) Administrative practices should be divorced from the time constraints and credit-hour bookkeeping that accompany normal academic life. (6) Program objectives and standards for progress should be competency-based, realistic, clearly defined, and closely monitored. (7) Student financial support should not be tied to progress toward a degree.

Promotion of Academic Progress. We have discussed limiting the scope of educational activities and the range of clients served within the existing funding constraints. Equally critical is attending to the quality of activities undertaken, which entails a serious effort to promote achievement and successful program completion for all students. What is most needed here is an effective advisement program so that students' progress through a coherent program of instruction is facilitated and monitored. Careful scheduling of courses would allow students to complete programs expediently. Enforced prerequisites should ensure appropriate sequencing of course work and allow advanced courses to focus realistically on advanced material. Rather than emphasizing course enrollments as the measure of success and basis for support, efforts should be made to establish course and program completions as indicators of effective community colleges, worthy of public financing.

A decision to focus on ensuring progress within delimited, quality programs would indirectly help stop the decline in critical literacy by encouraging both instructors and students to increase their commitment to the learning process. With clear educational goals and ongoing advisement, students would less likely be requirement meeters and more likely read and write extensively. Full-time faculty members with interested students to teach would be more likely to invest time in promoting texting. In addition, focusing on coherence and quality of overall instructional programs could lead to course objectives being refined to include higher-level cognitive objectives as well as affective objectives. This change, in itself, would lead to higher-level literacy demands.

Literacy development could be promoted directly as an essential aspect of academic achievement, but formulating standards for assessing literacy development will not be an easy task. The forms and functions of written language are changing rapidly. Our standards for assessing individual competencies remain firmly tied to the standardized examination developed in a cultural context that predates many current educational programs and forms of information transfer.

It can be argued that written language in our society is becoming better integrated with oral language as well as with other aspects of the social and physical setting. It would be strange indeed if Americans needed or developed the same reading and writing skills in a posttelevision era as they did when most information and entertainment came through the printed word. It would be equally peculiar if 60 percent of the population could be taught, and would find worth learning, the same type of literacy considered appropriate for 15 percent a generation ago. However, the literacy desirable today, though different in form, is still a *critical literacy*. We need to reconsider the current nature of critical literacy if our teaching of language skills is to become more powerful and functional for students and enhance their opportunities for success.

To define the reading and writing requirements to be promoted in each program area within the college, we need to establish literacy standards for admission to and completion of programs. Literacy standards could also be used as the basis for constructing instruments to identify and place students lacking in basic skills and to design instructional services to help them develop these skills. Such services could serve not only those admitted to programs and in need of academic support but also those who could not qualify for program admission. The success of each program in meeting its unique standards could be assessed by such indicators as program completion rates and the grade-point averages of its students in those courses with defined literacy standards.

Faculty Conditions. In the final analysis, administrators can affect the standards for literacy that prevail in classrooms only through actions that alter the characteristics and roles of faculty members and the conditions under which they teach. A first and obvious action involves reducing the number of part-time instructors. Leaving aside all issues relating to preparation and teaching ability of part-time versus full-time instructors, on which the evidence is far from clear, the growing use of part-time instructors can be associated with the deemphasis of critical literacy in several important ways.

First, large numbers of part-time instructors make the role of full-time instructors seem less important. This consequence was unintended, but it lessened faculty members' commitment to district priorities and shifted attention to outside interests. Such a loss of commitment or sense of responsibility to the organization has been documented by other researchers (Steers and Porter, 1979). With diminished faculty commitment and changing student characteristics, efficiency became the major criterion in assessing learning, a development that, in turn, led to the decreased demands for critical literacy.

Second, as a result of the increasing use of part-time staff, the number of students to be advised at Oakwood in relation to the number of full-time faculty members available for advising doubled during the ten years preceding the start of this study. Many of the inadequacies of the advisory system can be traced to this development. These inadequacies contributed to inappropriate course placements and the emphasis on requirement meeting that so inhibited the use of more complex reading and writing assignments.

Third, the loss of coherence in the curriculum was partly attributable to the dominance of part-time students and part-time instructors. The result was that full-time instructors voluntarily relinquished control over the curriculum; these faculty members found it more productive to concern themselves with discrete courses rather than sequences. Some programs were taught totally by part-time instructors, further contributing to the notion that developing and improving curricular sequences was a nonessential activity.

Apart from limiting the use of part-time instructors, administrators interested in encouraging critical literacy need to look at teaching loads and class size. The chair of the English department at Oakwood, who supervised twenty-seven faculty members and taught three sections of composition one semester and four the other, was not a good candidate for leading a resurgence of emphasis on written expression. Faculty members who taught overloads while carrying standard fifteen-hour loads needed efficient bitting strategies from their students in order to survive. Advanced sections that offered no relief from the minimum enrollments required for introductory sections discouraged the use of written assignments as well. Teaching loads and class sizes will have to be set with explicit understanding of the literacy goals to be pursued and the conditions necessary for their achievement.

Last but not least, if promoting critical literacy is to be a priority, community colleges will need more full-time instructors who are trained to teach basic skills and who know how they can be taught in tandem with required content. In addition, staff development and faculty support services will be needed to help faculty members deal with the demands of encouraging critical literacy. Faculty members must feel an institutional commitment to critical literacy if they are to be expected to take on the challenge of developing it within their classrooms.

A Final Word

The declining emphasis on critical literacy in community colleges is related in complex ways to current priorities. Even if colleges make a commitment to promoting more complex literacy behaviors, they will have to develop interrelated strategies for coordinating the necessary policy changes. Equally important, they will have to reestablish the importance of degree attainment in an institution dominated by part-time students meeting the requirements of discrete courses. Sound advising and program coherence are indispensable to those wanting to earn a degree. Even those uninterested in degrees will not be harmed by such assistance. Open-access colleges need to again emphasize advising and program coherence instead of strategies to enroll as many part-time students as possible in discrete courses.

Community colleges can promote critical literacy to students with realistic academic or occupational goals, or they can offer a broad range of content through efficient bitting procedures to everyone who shows up in response to their advertising. The evidence to date indicates they cannot do both and encourage the standards of individual performance on critical literacy tasks that characterized an earlier era with a less cluttered curriculum. The choice of relative emphasis is a matter for public policy.

References

Akinnaso, F. N. "The Consequences of Literacy in Pragmatic and Theoretical Perspectives." *Anthropology and Education Quarterly,* 1981, *12,* 163–200.

Amidon, E., and Hunter, E. *Improving Teaching: The Analysis of Classroom Interaction.* New York: Holt, Rinehart and Winston, 1967.

Arwardy, J. W., and Chafin, C. K. "The Transitional Curriculum Program: Toward Learner Independence Through Developmental Education." Paper presented at the National Developmental Studies Conference, Atlanta, November 1980. (ERIC Document Reproduction Service No. ED 197 662)

Astin, A. W. *Four Critical Years: Effects of College on Beliefs, Attitudes, and Knowledge.* San Francisco: Jossey-Bass, 1977.

Astin, A. W. *Minorities in American Higher Education.* San Francisco: Jossey-Bass, 1982.

171

Attinasi, L. C., Stahl, V. V., and Okun, M. A. "A Preliminary Typology of Motivational Orientations of Community College Students." *Community/Junior College*, 1982, *6*(4), 371-490.

Berg, I. *Education and Training: The Great Training Robbery.* New York: Praeger, 1970.

Bertalanffy, L. *A Systems View of Man: Collected Essays.* Boulder, Colo.: Westview Press, 1981.

Bloom, B. S. (Ed.). *Taxonomy of Educational Objectives.* Handbook I: *Cognitive Domain.* New York: McKay, 1956.

Bloome, D. "Reading and Writing in a Classroom: A Sociolinguistic Ethnography." Paper presented at the meeting of the American Education Research Association, Los Angeles, April 1981.

Bormuth, J. R. "Value and Volume of Literacy." *Visible Language,* 1978, *12*, 118-161.

Boshier, R. "Motivational Orientations of Adult Education Participants: A Factor Analytic Exploration of Houle's Typology." *Adult Education,* 1971, *21*, 3-26.

Boshier, R. "Educational Participation and Dropout: A Theoretical Model." *Adult Education,* 1973, *23*, 255-282.

Boshier, R. "Motivational Orientations Revisited: Life-Span Motives and the Education Participation Scale." *Adult Education,* 1977, *27*, 89-115.

Boyer, E. L., and Hechinger, F. *Higher Learning in the Nation's Service.* Washington, D.C.: Carnegie Foundation for the Advancement of Teaching, 1981.

Boyer, E. L., and Kaplan, M. *Educating for Survival.* New Rochelle, N.Y.: Change Magazine Press, 1977.

Brann, E. T. H. *Paradoxes of Education in a Republic.* Chicago: University of Chicago Press, 1979.

Breneman, D. W., and Nelson, S. C. *Financing Community Colleges: An Economic Perspective.* Washington, D.C.: Brookings Institute, 1981.

Burnett, J. H. "Event Description and Analysis in the Microethnography of Urban Classrooms." In I. F. Lanni and E. Storey (Eds.), *Cultural Relevance and Educational Issues.* Boston: Little, Brown, 1973.

California Postsecondary Education Commission. "Missions and

Functions of the California Community Colleges." Unpublished paper, Sacramento, Calif., May 1981.

Carnegie Commission on Higher Education. *A Chance to Learn.* New York: McGraw-Hill, 1970.

Carnegie Foundation for the Advancement of Teaching. *Missions of the College Curriculum: A Contemporary Review with Suggestions.* San Francisco: Jossey-Bass, 1977.

Center for the Study of Community Colleges. "Report of Instructor Surveys, 1977–1978." Unpublished report, 1978a.

Center for the Study of Community Colleges. "Science and Humanities Instruction in Two-Year Colleges." Unpublished report, 1978b.

Clark, B. R. *The Open Door College: A Case Study.* New York: McGraw-Hill, 1960.

Cohen, A. M. "Ten Criticisms of Developmental Education." *Junior College Resource Review,* Spring 1982, 17–19.

Cohen, A. M., and Brawer, F. B. "Instructional Practices in the Humanities and Sciences." Unpublished report, Center for the Study of Community Colleges, 1981.

Cohen, A. M., and Brawer, F. B. *The American Community College.* San Francisco: Jossey-Bass, 1982.

Cole, M., and Scribner, S. "Cross-Cultural Studies of Memory and Cognition." In R. V. Kail and J. W. Hagen (Eds.), *Perspectives on the Development of Memory and Cognition.* Hillsdale, N.J.: Erlbaum, 1977.

Cooper, C. R. "Different Ways of Being a Teacher: An Ethnographic Study of a College Instructor's Academic and Social Roles in the Classroom." *Journal of Classroom Interaction,* 1981a, *16*(2), 27–37.

Cooper, C. R. "An Ethnographic Study of Teaching Style." 1981b. (ERIC Document Reproduction Service No. ED 209 213)

Coppermann, P. *The Literacy Hoax: The Decline of Reading, Writing, and Learning in the Public Schools and What We Can Do About It.* New York: Morrow, 1978.

Covelli, N. J. "Shifts in Student Enrollments and Their Effects on the Institutional Management of Gateway Technical Institute." Unpublished doctoral dissertation, Nova University,

1979. (ERIC Document Reproduction Service No. ED 013 371)

Cross, K. P. *Accent on Learning: Improving Instruction and Reshaping the Curriculum.* San Francisco: Jossey-Bass, 1976.

Cytrynbaum, S., and Conran, P. C. "Impediments to the Process of Learning." *Illinois School Research and Development,* 1979, *15*(2), 49–65.

Delamont, S. "Beyond Flanders Field: The Relationship of Subject Matter and Individuality to Classroom Style." In M. Stubbs and S. Delamont (Eds.), *Explorations in Classroom Observation.* New York: Wiley, 1976.

Dreyfus, A., and Eggleston, J. F. "Classroom Transactions of Student-Teachers of Science." *European Journal of Science Education,* 1979, *1*(3), 315–325.

Dubois, B. L. Review of *The Language Makers* by Roy Harris. *Language Learning,* 1980, *30,* 497–499.

Eisenstein, E. L. "The Emergence of Print Culture in the West." *Journal of Communication,* 1980, *30,* 99–106.

Eison, J. A. "A New Instrument for Assessing Students' Orientations Towards Grades and Learning." *Psychological Reports,* 1981, *48,* 919–924.

Erickson, F., and Schultz, J. "When Is a Context? Some Issues and Methods in the Analysis of Social Competence." In J. Green and C. Wallet (Eds.), *Ethnography and Language in Educational Settings.* Norwood, N.J.: Ablex, 1981.

Feldman, R. S., and Prohaska, T. "The Student as Pygmalion: Effect of Student Expectation on the Teacher." *Journal of Educational Psychology,* 1979, *71*(4), 485–493.

Flanders, N. *Analyzing Teacher Behavior.* Reading, Mass.: Addison-Wesley, 1970.

Freire, P. *Pedagogy of the Oppressed.* New York: Seabury Press, 1968.

Freire, P. "The People Speak Their Word: Learning to Read and Write in Sao Tome and Principe." *Harvard Educational Review,* 1981, *51*(1), 27–30.

Fund for the Improvement of Postsecondary Education. *FY 1974 Program Information.* Washington, D.C.: Department of Health, Education and Welfare, 1973.

Furlong, V. A., and Edwards, A. D. "Language in Classroom Interaction: Theory and Data." *Educational Research,* 1977, *19,* 122-128.

Garrison, R. H. *Junior College Faculty: Issues and Problems. A Preliminary National Appraisal.* Washington, D.C.: American Association of Junior Colleges, 1967. (ERIC Document Reproduction Service No. ED 012 177)

Gilmore, P., and Smith, D. M. (Eds.). *Children in and out of School: Ethnography and Education.* Washington, D.C.: Center for Applied Linguistics, 1982.

Glendale Community College General Catalog: 1966-1967. Glendale, Ariz.: Glendale Community College, 1966.

Goody, J. *The Domestication of the Savage Mind.* Cambridge: Cambridge University Press, 1977.

Graff, H. J. *The Literacy Myth: Literacy and Social Structure in the Nineteenth Century City.* New York: Academic Press, 1979.

Grede, J., and Friedlander, J. "Adult Basic Education in Community Colleges." *Junior College Resource Review,* 1981. (ERIC Document Reproduction Service No. ED 207 649)

Green, J., and Wallat, C. (Ed.). *Ethnography and Language in Educational Settings.* Norwood, N.J.: Ablex, 1981.

Harrow, A. J. *A Taxonomy of the Psychomotor Domain.* New York: McKay, 1972.

Havelock, E. *Origins of Western Literacy.* Toronto: Ontario Institute for Studies in Education, 1976.

Havighurst, R. J. "Education Through the Adult Life Span." *Educational Gerontology,* 1976, *1,* 41-51.

Heath, S. B. "Protean Shapes in Literacy Events: Ever-Shifting Oral and Literate Traditions." In D. Tannen (Ed.), *Spoken and Written Language.* Norwood, N.J.: Ablex, 1982.

Hirschman, A. O. *Exit, Voice, and Loyalty: Responses to Declines In Firms, Organizations and States.* Cambridge: Harvard University Press, 1970.

Houle, C. O. *The Inquiring Mind.* Madison: University of Wisconsin, 1961.

Hymes, D. "Introduction: Toward Ethnographics of Communication." *American Anthropologist,* 1964, *66,* 1-34.

Jacob, E., and Crandall, J. A. "Job-Related Literacy: A Look at Current and Needed Research." Unpublished paper, Center for Applied Linguistics, Washington, D.C., 1979.

Jencks, C., and Riesman, D. *The Academic Revolution.* Garden City, N.Y.: Doubleday, 1968.

Johnson, G. R., and McNamara, J. F. "Do Disciplines Differ in Their Verbal Interactions Within the College Classroom?" Unpublished paper, Texas A&M University, 1980.

Karabel, J. "Community Colleges and Social Stratification." *Harvard Educational Review,* 1972a, *42*(4), 521-561.

Karabel, J. "Open Admissions: Toward Meritocracy or Democracy?" *Change,* 1972b, *4*(4), 38-43.

Karabel, J. "Protecting the Portals: Class and the Community College." *Social Policy,* 1974, *5*(1), 12-18.

Kirst, M. "Report to the Policy Committee on the University of California's Activities to Assist Underprepared Students." Paper prepared for the College Board Project Equality Symposium, St. Louis, May 1981.

Kissler, G. R. "Report of the Task Group on Retention and Transfer." Unpublished report, University of California at Berkeley, 1980.

Knowles, M. *The Adult Learner: A Neglected Species.* Houston: Gulf, 1978.

Koehler, V. "Classroom Process Research: Present and Future." *Journal of Classroom Interaction,* 1978, *13*(2), 3-11.

Krathwohl, D. R., Bloom, B. S., and Masia, B. B. *Taxonomy of Educational Objectives.* Handbook 2: *Affective Domain.* New York: McKay, 1964.

Kuhn, T. *The Structure of Scientific Revolutions.* Chicago: University of Chicago Press, 1970.

Kurth, E. L., and Mills, E. R. *Analysis of Degree of Faculty Satisfaction in Florida Community Colleges.* Final Report. Gainesville: Institute of Higher Education, University of Florida, 1968. (ERIC Document Reproduction Service No. 027 902)

Leont'ev, A. N. "The Problem of Activity in Soviet Psychology." *Soviet Psychology,* 1974, *13*, 4-33.

Logan, M., and Van Fleet, A. A. "Student and Faculty Culture in Higher Education: A Research Note." *Journal of Thought,* 1980, *15*(3), 77-80.

London, H. B. *The Culture of a Community College.* New York: Praeger, 1978.

McCabe, R. H., and Skidmore, S. "The Literacy Crisis and American Education." *Junior College Resource Review,* Spring 1982, 2-6.

Mann, R. D., and others. *The College Classroom: Conflict, Change, and Learning.* New York: Wiley, 1970.

Meacham, J. A. "A Dialectical Approach to Moral Judgment and Self-Esteem." *Human Development,* 1975, *18,* 159-170.

Mehan, H. "Structuring School Structure." *Educational Review,* 1978, *48,* 32-64.

Mikulecky, L., and Diehl, N. *Job Literacy.* Reading Research Center Technical Report. Bloomington: Indiana University, 1979.

Moore, W. *Community College Response to the High Risk Student: A Critical Reappraisal.* ERIC Clearinghouse for Junior Colleges, Horizon Series. Washington, D.C.: American Association of Community and Junior Colleges, 1976.

Morrill, W. T., and Steffy, D. M. "The Ethnography of Collegiate Teaching: Bridging the Student and Academic Cultures." *Journal of Thought,* 1980, *15*(3), 49-76.

Morrison, J. C., and Ferrante, R. *Compensatory Education in Two-Year Colleges.* University Park: Center for the Study of Higher Education, Pennsylvania State University, 1973.

National Assessment of Educational Progress. *Reading, Thinking and Writing: Results from the 1979-80 National Assessment of Reading and Literature.* Denver, Colo.: National Assessment of Educational Progress, 1981.

Neumann, W., and Riesman, D. "The Community College Elite." In G. B. Vaughan (Ed.), *New Directions for Community Colleges: Questioning the Community College Role,* no. 32. San Francisco: Jossey-Bass, 1980.

O'Banion, T. *New Directions in Community College Student Personnel Programs.* Student Personnel Series, no. 15. Washington, D.C.: American College Personnel Association, 1971.

Ogbu, J. U. "School Ethnography: A Multilevel Approach." *Anthropology and Education Quarterly,* 1981, *12,* 3-27.

Olivas, M. A. *The Dilemma of Access: Minorities in Two-Year Colleges.* Washington, D.C.: Howard University Press, 1979.

Olson, D. R. "From Utterance to Text: The Bias of Language in Speech and Writing." *Harvard Educational Review,* 1977, *47*(3), 257-281.

Ong, W. J. "Literacy and Orality in Our Times." *Journal of Communication,* 1980, *30,* 197-204.

Philips, S. U. "Participant Structures and Communicative Competence: Warm Springs Children in Community and Classroom." In C. Cazden, V. John, and D. Hymes (Eds.), *Functions of Language in the Classroom.* New York: Teachers College Press, 1972.

Pincus, F. L. "The False Promises of Community Colleges: Class Conflict and Vocational Education." *Harvard Educational Review,* 1980, *50*(3), 332-361.

Resnick, D. P., and Resnick, L. B. "The Nature of Literacy: An Historical Exploration." *Harvard Educational Review,* 1977, *47*(3), 370-385.

Richardson, R. C., Jr., and Leslie, L. L. *The Impossible Dream? Financing Community College's Evolving Mission.* Washington, D.C.: AACJC/CVC/ERIC Clearinghouse for Junior Colleges, 1980.

Richardson, R. C., and others. "A Report of Literacy Development in Community Colleges: Technical Report." National Institute of Education, 1982. (ERIC Document Reproduction Service No. ED 217 925)

Roueche, J. E., and Snow, J. J. *Overcoming Learning Problems: A Guide to Developmental Education in College.* San Francisco: Jossey-Bass, 1977.

Roueche, S. D., and Comstock, U. N. "A Report on Theory and Methods for the Study of Literacy Development in Community Colleges." National Institute of Education, 1981. (ERIC Document Reproduction Service No. ED 211 161)

Rue, R. "Please Do Not Apply: Turning Them Away from the Community College." *Change,* 1982, *14*(8), 12.

Salancik, G. B. "Commitment and the Control of Organizational Behavior and Beliefs." In B. M. Staw and G. R. Salancik

(Eds.), *New Directions in Organizational Behavior.* Chicago: St. Clair, 1977.

Scollon, R., and Scollon, S. *Narrative, Literacy, and Face in Interethnic Communication.* Norwood, N.J.: Ablex, 1981.

Scribner, S., and Cole, M. *The Psychology of Literacy.* Cambridge, Mass.: Harvard University Press, 1981.

Scribner, S., and Jacob, E. *Industrial Literacy Project.* Progress Report. Washington, D.C.: Center for Applied Linguistics, 1980.

Shor, I. *Critical Teaching and Everyday Life.* Boston: South End Press, 1980.

Steers, R. M., and Porter, L. W. (Eds.). *Motivation and Work Behavior.* New York: McGraw-Hill, 1979.

Sticht, T. G. (Ed.). *Reading for Working: A Functional Literacy Anthology.* Alexandria, Va.: Human Resources Research Organization, 1975.

Sticht, T. G. "Developing Literacy and Learning Strategies in Organizational Settings." In H. F. O'Neil (Ed.), *Learning Strategies: Issues and Procedures.* New York: Academic Press, 1978.

Stiles, W. B., and others. "Professorial Presumptions in Verbal Interactions with University Students." *Journal of Experimental Social Psychology,* 1979, *15*(2), 158–169.

Vygotsky, L. S. *Thought and Language.* (L. E. Haufmann and G. Vakar, Trans.) Cambridge, Mass.: M.I.T. Press, 1962.

Watts, L. K. "Social Interaction in the Classroom." Working paper, Literacy in the Community College Project, Arizona State University, 1981.

Whiteman, M. F. *Writing: The Nature, Development, and Teaching of Written Communication.* Vol. 1: *Variation in Writing: Functional and Linguistic-Cultural Differences.* 1981. (ERIC Document Reproduction Service No. ED 214 204)

Wilkinson, L. C. (Ed.). *Communicating in the Classroom.* New York: Academic Press, 1981.

Wilms, W. W. *Public and Proprietary Vocational Training: A Study of Effectiveness.* Lexington, Mass.: Lexington Books, 1975.

Wilms, W. W. *Vocational Education and Social Mobility: A Study of Public and Proprietary School Dropouts and Graduates.* Los Angeles: Graduate School of Education, University of California, 1980.

Yarrington, R. "Overview: Literacy in Community Colleges." *Junior College Resource Review,* Spring 1982, 1-2.

Zwerling, L. S. *Second Best: The Crisis of the Community College.* New York: McGraw-Hill, 1976.

Index

A

Academic progress, and critical literacy, 158, 165-167

Administration: analysis of priorities of, 120-145; and change and conflict, 143-144; and decision making, 121-124; and facilities expansion, 132-133, 138; and instructor's adaptations, 82-83; at Oakwood College, 28-33; and planning and resource allocation, 126-128, 131-134; and reorganization and staffing changes, 124-126, 131; of Richfield District, 17-20; and staff development, 128-129; strategies of, 124-134; values of, 138-140

Admissions and placement, and critical literacy, 158, 159-161

Advisement: academic, changes in, 108-112; and academic progress, 166; faculty involvement with, 110-112; and literacy, 106-112; and orientation, 107-108

Affective domain: concept of, 74; difficulties of, 77-78

Akinnaso, F. N., 4, 8, 171

Amidon, E., 43, 171

Anecdotal lectures, and information-transfer courses, 49-50

Arizona State University, xi

Arwardy, J. W., 84, 171

Astin, A. W., 11-12, 160, 171

Attentive audience: as requirement meeters, 90; as student style, 48

181